THIS BOOK IS ANTI-RACIST

BY TIFFANY JEWELL
ILLUSTRATED BY AURÉLIA DURAND

Frances Lincoln
Children's Books

AUTHOR'S NOTE

You will notice I have chosen to use "folx" instead of "folks" because it is a ***gender*** *neutral term created by activist communities, and I would like to honor everyone who reads this book. Replacing the "ks" with an "x" allows for every reader who has never been seen before to see themselves in here. We'll capitalize Black, Brown, Indigenous, People of Color, and* ***Folx of the Global Majority*** *because I believe it is important to center the voices and lives of those who have been* ***marginalized****, silenced, and purposefully left out of our history for so long. I am building solidarity in the language I choose.*

I do not use the term "minority" to describe Black, Brown, and Indigenous folx because we are the majority in the world. Using the language of racism can minimize our full selves. It can allow us to forget our deepest roots and ancestors; it allows us to create a history that, while in our own voices, has been shaped by the oppressor.

Because ***race*** *and our social identities are constructed by people (and often those with the* ***privilege*** *of having academia to back them up), we are still often caught in the trap of labeling ourselves in ways that center whiteness and those in the dominant culture. I ask you, when possible, please use the names and language that honor you, your family, and your history. Please use the names and language that honor those who are continually silenced and ignored, those who are renamed and have been stripped of their histories. Reclaim the language and names that were stolen and lost over decades.*

To all of you,

I wrote this book for you. It's for everyone. The words on these pages are for our ancestors and those who should not yet be our ancestors, but who passed on too soon. I wrote this for you out of a love for liberation and our humanity.

This is the book I wish I'd had when I was younger. And it's the book I will share with my own children. It contains information I never learned when I was younger and you will probably not be taught in school.

I wrote these words for you while carrying a heavy heart. It aches for Emmett Till, Tamir Rice, Korryn Gaines, Michael Brown, Eric Garner, Sandra Bland, Bobby Hutton, Antwon Rose Jr., Stephon Clark, Rekia Boyd, Stephen Lawrence, Charleena Lyles, Alton Sterling, Philando Castile, Aiyana Stanley-Jones, and Trayvon Martin, and for all those who we honor with hashtags, our tears, our frustration and rage, our exhaustion and the fire to move on.

My optimism has brought me to action and to sharing these words with you because I believe you will help to dismantle and work toward ending racism. We need justice. No one's names should be memorialized in hashtags.

My hope is you will use this book as a way to start your journey in the big work of anti-racism. You are resisting racism and oppression just by opening these pages. You are entering into a consciousness that wakes you up and allows you to see the world in a whole new way.

Some may tell you you're too young to talk about race. People may tell you that you should stop talking about skin color and see everyone as a "global citizen." You may have been told racism isn't a problem any more and that calling it out or bringing it up in conversation is wrong. Some people may have given you the impression that you are wrong and stirring up trouble. You are not! Racism is a problem, a very serious problem, and it needs to be talked about because it isn't going away if we do nothing. It is okay for you to continue on with this book and I am so proud of you for picking this up and opening these pages.

Please know you are not alone on this journey. I am here with you. There are many, many folx who are here with you, who came before you, and who will come long after us. I hope you will share this book with your friends and families because fighting racism really isn't something you can do all on your own. Make sure to look up **underlined words** in the glossary if you need help understanding.

There are many moments to pause in this book so you can check in with yourself and grow into your activism. You will learn more about yourself, our history, how racism came to be, and why we're still so deep within it. We will work together, in solidarity, to disrupt racism and become anti-racist accomplices. This book is meant to be read in order. Each chapter builds on the previous chapter and you will gain a deeper understanding of becoming your anti-racist self. And you will probably want to read and reread this. This is a start. Anti-racism is lifelong work.

In solidarity,
Tiffany

ANTI-RACIST

An **ANTI-RACIST** person is someone who is opposed to racism.

Anti-racism is actively working against racism. It is making a commitment to resisting unjust laws, policies, and racist attitudes. Anti-racism is how we get free from centuries of living in a racialized society that keeps us separate and oppressed.

IN THIS SECTION:
• WHO AM I?
• WHAT ARE MY SOCIAL IDENTITIES?
• WHAT IS RACE?
• WHAT IS RACISM?
GIRLS
BE FIERCE

WAKING UP

UNDERSTANDING AND GROWING INTO MY IDENTITIES

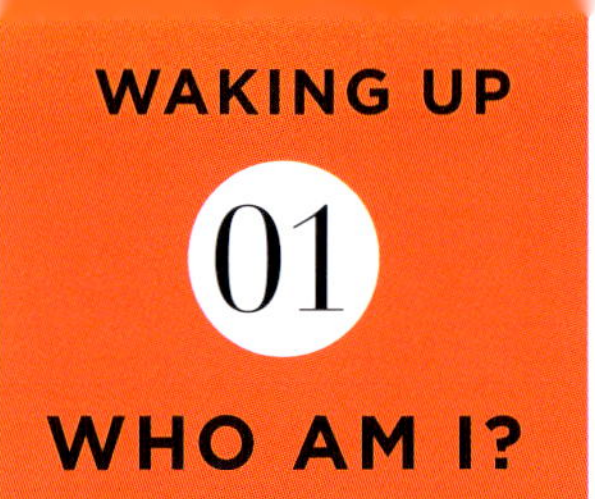

Who are you?

You are *you*.

You are the only you there is. There's so much that makes you who you are. Your identity is what makes you, **YOU**: it's all the parts that make you unique.

You are made up of your family, your friends, your neighborhood, your school, what you see on social media and read in books, what you hear and listen to, what you eat, what you wear, what you feel, your dreams, the stories you cannot wait to share and those you don't want to tell and everything in between and all around.

YOU ARE EVERYTHING WITHIN YOU AND EVERYTHING THAT SURROUNDS YOU.

You are all the ancestors who came before you: those you've never known, never heard of, never seen—and those you've passed on the street, sat next to, and snuggled near.

I'm sure you've asked, **"WHO AM I?"** and others have asked, **"WHO ARE YOU?"**

How do you answer? How much of yourself do you share with others—if anything? This is who I was at 14...

I'M
TIFFANY.

I'M 14 YEARS OLD.

I LIVE IN A SMALL HOUSE IN NEW YORK STATE. I LIVE WITH MY MOM AND MY TWIN SISTER. I'M A BLACK BIRACIAL CISGENDER FEMALE WHO HAS BROWN EYES AND A LOT OF FRECKLES. I HAVE CURLY HAIR AND HAVE GROWN TO LOVE IT, SLOWLY, OVER TIME. I LOVE TO READ AND BAKE. I LOVE TO DANCE WITH MY FRIENDS AND I WRITE TERRIBLE POETRY THAT ONLY I WILL EVER READ. ALL OF THAT IS WHO I AM...

AND I'M SO MUCH MORE.

YOU get to decide which identities you will share with the world and how you'll do so. You get to choose how to name your identities.

Your identity grows and changes just like you. There are some things that are static and stay with you always. My skin color and the many freckles on my face have been with me for as long as I can remember and will continue on with me until I am 103+!

There are other parts of us that change (even daily). I can wear my hair up or down, braided or straight; I can change the color and the length—it's all up to me.

MANY OTHERS WILL TRY TO GET YOU TO FIT INTO AN IMAGINARY BOX.

This box includes what we call "the dominant culture." If you are white, upper middle class, **cisgender** male, educated, athletic, **neurotypical**, and/or able-bodied, you are in this box. (We'll go through all of these in the next chapter.)

If you do not fit into this box, you are considered to be a part of what's called the "subordinate culture." Folx included in the "subordinate culture", include Black, Brown, Indigenous People of Color of the Global Majority, queer, **transgender**, and **nonbinary** folx, and cisgender women, youth, Muslim, Jewish, Buddhist, atheist, and non-Christian folx, **neurodiverse** folx, folx living with disabilities, those living in poverty, and more. There are many more who exist outside of this imaginary box than those who fit inside of it.

The dominant culture is what has been considered "normal" and this "normal" has been created and is maintained by those who are in the box. It is this version of normal that has shaped how we see ourselves and the world around us.

Who is smart? Beautiful? Worthy? A leader? Trouble?

Many labels and descriptions have been created so it seems like people either fit neatly into the box or not. I never really did. And you don't need to either.

Our many identities make us who we are. They help others to understand who you are and help you to know more about the folx who are in your life and in the world. They connect us and divide us. Understanding who you are allows you to grow and know more about yourself. It can give you direction and empower you. The world will try to tell you who you are, but you are the only person who gets to decide that.

YOU HAVE THE RIGHT TO BE SEEN AND UNDERSTOOD WITHOUT HAVING TO COMPROMISE WHO YOU ARE.

Activity:

1. Pull out a notebook. (Make sure it's a notebook you'll want to keep coming back to, one that you can carry around with you.) For the next five minutes, write down everything you can think of that makes you who you are.

You're creating a list of your identities!

I am...

Female, cis female
Black biracial
Light skinned
A twin
A daughter
A first-generation American
A bread baker
Freckled
Tall and thin
A sister
Curly haired
English and American
An English speaker
A side sleeper
Allergic
A reader

A creator
Glasses wearer
A comfy-clothes wearer
A chocolate lover
Stubborn
Resistant
Optimistic
An extrovert who needs some recharge time
Always cold
A drama kid
Always right (at least, I want to be...)
Confusing to others

2.

Create **your identity map**.
Grab a piece of plain paper,
or continue in your notebook.
Write your name in the center and,
from there, place your identities all
around you. Feel free to illustrate,
as this is your map.

DOMINANT CULTURE

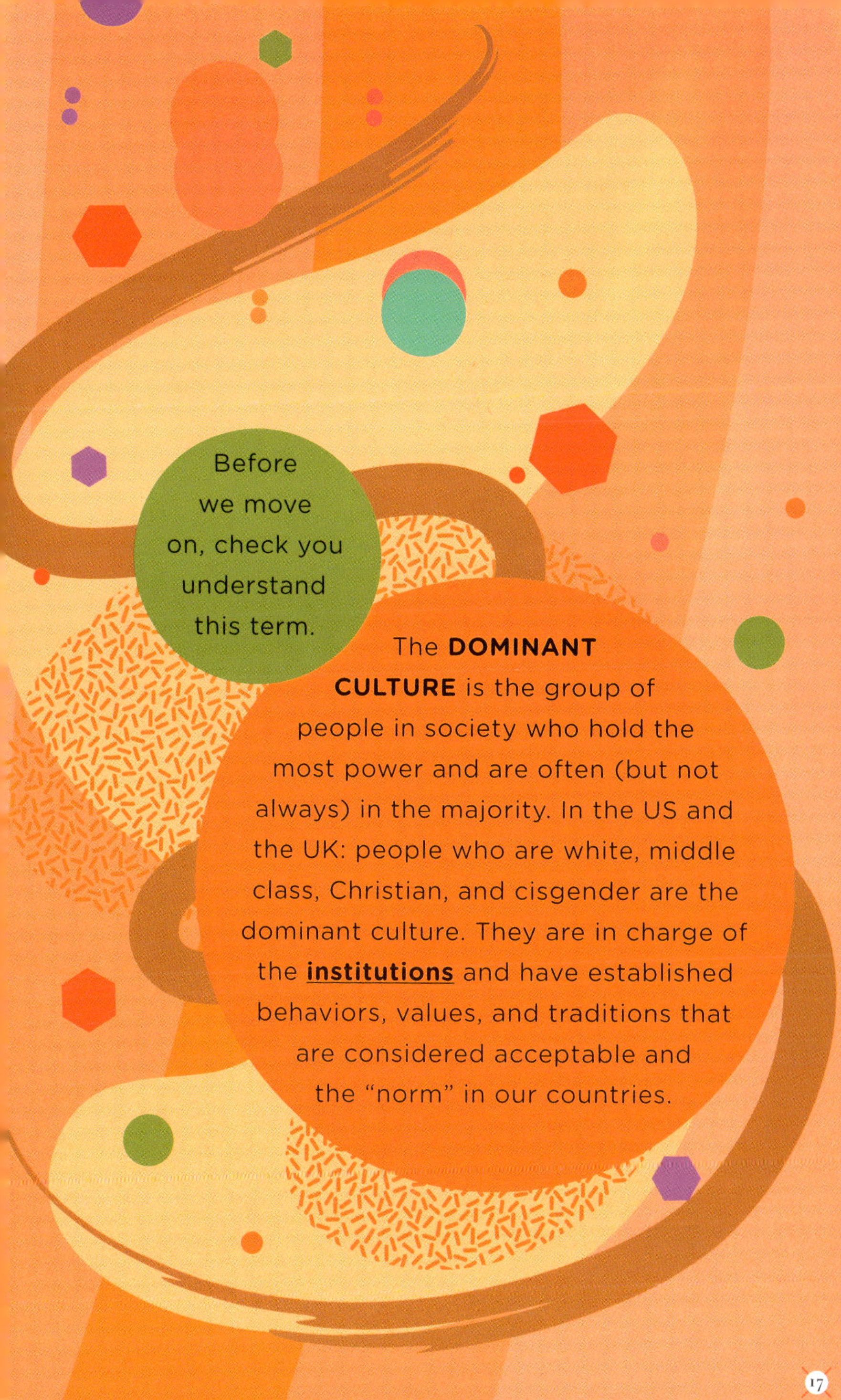

Before we move on, check you understand this term.

The **DOMINANT CULTURE** is the group of people in society who hold the most power and are often (but not always) in the majority. In the US and the UK: people who are white, middle class, Christian, and cisgender are the dominant culture. They are in charge of the **institutions** and have established behaviors, values, and traditions that are considered acceptable and the "norm" in our countries.

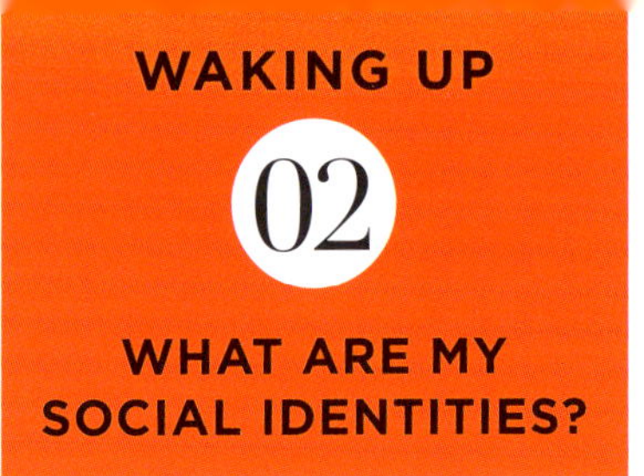

YOUR MANY IDENTITIES ARE PARTS OF THE WHOLE YOU: ONE PART ALONE DOES NOT DEFINE WHO YOU ARE.

Some of those parts you create for yourself. Other parts of your identity have been created by society. **"SOCIETY"** is another way of saying community. These identities have been created, named, framed, and defined by society for a very long time. We call them **"SOCIAL IDENTITIES."** Your social identity is the you that relates to other people in society (for example, your neighborhood, city, or country). Much of our culture comes from our social identities and the groups we belong to.

CATEGORIES

Our social identities are broken down into groups, or categories, that we get lumped into. This is not always our choice. Others may place you in categories even though you may not identify in the same way. This is a way of trying to figure you and others like you out. It is how our communities and countries have been set up for centuries. While the social identity categories can help us to see and understand ourselves and the people around us, they also determine how others will treat us. It is our job to learn and act.

First ask: What are these social identities and why do they exist? Analyze them with a critical and conscious eye, and then work to undo why this is our current situation.

YOU HAVE
THE ABILITY
TO CREATE
A NEW
HISTORY

In this book we will focus mostly on our racial identities. But there are many categories within our identities that affect the way we interact with society. You may be familiar with the following:

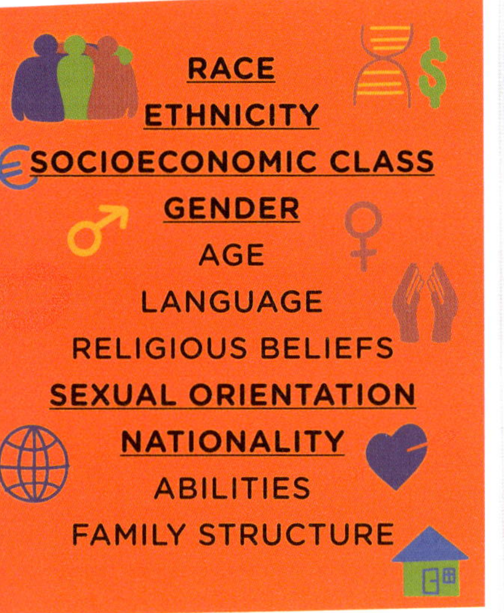

The parts of your identity that you notice and are most aware of on a daily basis may change depending on where you are, who you are with, and the experiences you continue to have in life. The identities you do not think much about, even the ones you barely notice, are always with you.

PRIVILEGE

Some social identities hold power and privilege, others do not. Even within us, there are parts of us that hold some power and other parts that are oppressed. This is why we work to understand our identities within society; we need to always examine our whole selves. The identities that fit neatly into the imaginary box are typically the ones with the most power and **agency**.

One example of where I have some power is the language I speak. I live in a country where the most commonly spoken language is English. I can read and understand signs and directions. I can walk into a school or store and the folx helping me will likely know what I'm talking about. I don't have to worry.

Privilege is the benefits you receive due to how close you are to the dominant culture. For example: a white, cisgender man, who is able-bodied, **heterosexual**, considered handsome, and speaks English has more privilege than a Black transgender woman. Those with privilege have power over others. Not everyone has privilege. Folx who do not benefit from their social identities, who are in the subordinate culture, have little to no privilege and power.

Some of our identities hold privileges and disadvantages at the same time. Because I am cis female, I don't have to think about which restroom I will be able to use. I have agency.

But because I am female, I do not have the same privileges a **cis male** has. I am more likely to be overlooked for a position of leadership and get paid less for the same amount of work. While many cis heterosexual men can confidently walk alone at night, I cannot without feeling some fear that I may be harmed.

Although I do not have the same privileges as a white cisgender male, I do have privileges trans and nonbinary folx do not have because my **cisgender identity** is closer to the dominant culture.

INTERSECTIONALITY

Looking at intersectionality helps us to understand how our social identities affect our whole life. Kimberlé Crenshaw, a Black female lawyer, author, scholar, and civil rights activist, used the term intersectionality in 1989 to help us better understand that being a woman AND Black created greater disadvantages than just being a woman.

A Black woman is **marginalized** because she is a woman and because she is Black. Her experiences overlap and cause great harm. When you just look at a person through a single lens you can only narrowly understand them and their experiences.

WHEN YOU LOOK AT ALL OF THE PARTS OF A PERSON AND WHERE THEY ARE OPPRESSED, YOU WILL BETTER UNDERSTAND HOW DEEPLY DISCRIMINATION ADVANCES ONWARD.

Knowing who we are, where we hold agency, how our identities came to be, and how they determine our roles in society helps us to understand ourselves and how we can change a system where some folx have privilege and power, and some folx are under-resourced and oppressed, to one where we are all liberated. (We will learn more about privilege in chapters 15 and 17.)

Activity:

Pull out your notebook. Create a list of the **social identity categories** we mentioned in this chapter. Can you think of more? Now write down your identity within those socially constructed categories.

Reflect:

What do you notice? Are there parts of you that hold power and privilege within your community? Are there parts of your identity that exist outside of the dominant culture?

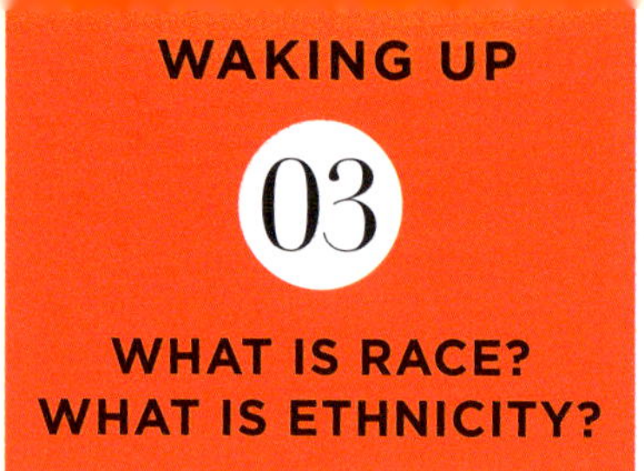

In this book, when we talk about race, we are referring to our skin color. People have been divided for centuries based on the differences in skin tone, hair texture, facial features, and cultural heritage.

> *THE CONCEPT OF RACE IS NOT ACTUALLY BASED ON SCIENCE, IT IS A CREATION OF SOCIETY.*

The categories for race have been created, over many years, by people in the dominant culture. In the mid-1700s, European scientists started to classify people just as they categorized plants and animals. We still study some of them, like Carl Linnaeus and Johann Friedrich Blumenbach, in our schools today.[1] Their "science" created a hierarchy of humans, which placed Europeans with the lightest skin at the top. Indigenous folx and those with the darkest skin were not valued.

The racial categories we get lumped into in the US include: White, Black (or African American), Asian, American Indian or Alaska Native (or Indigenous), Native Hawaiian or Pacific Islander, and Multiracial (also called Biracial or Mixed).

Your skin color, along with many of your characteristics, were passed down to you from generation to generation. Folx with African ancestry have more melanin than those with European ancestry. Melanin is the pigment in our skin that protects us

from the UV rays of the sun and takes in vitamin D.

The term "white" includes people with ancestors from Europe, in particular, Northern Europe. They have the least amount of pigmentation. The term Black includes folx with ancestors mainly from Africa (this includes African Americans, folx from Jamaica, the Dominican Republic, Haiti, and other countries in the Caribbean.) They have more melanin because they live closer to the equator, where there is more sunlight. The term Brown includes folx with Asian and/or **Latinx** ancestry.[2] Indigenous refers to folx whose ancestors were the first people in a particular land or area. Biracial and multiracial folx have ancestry from two or more different racial categories.

ETHNICITY

Race often gets confused with ethnicity. Your ethnic identity is your cultural identity. This is also a **social construction**. Unlike race, which specifically looks at your physical features, ethnicity zeroes in on your family's cultural and ancestral heritage—like language, traditions, and history—to place you into categories. Some examples of ethnicities are: Japanese American, Caribbean Navajo, and Sudanese. Often, where you are from will partly determine your ethnicity.

The names for these divisions, as well as the definition of race, have changed, and continue to do so. For example, in the past, people used the term Caucasian to refer to those with a lack of melanin. The word was popularized in the late 1800s by the German **anthropologist** we mentioned earlier, Johann Friedrich Blumenbach. He referred to Europeans and the people who lived in the Caucasus region as "the most beautiful race of men."[3] (This, of course, was based on his opinion and not on scientific data.) So, in this book, we will refer to white people as white.

Another example of how the names of the categories have changed is the term "mulatto." When I was a kid, many folx (including teachers and family) referred to me using that word rather than calling me biracial. "Mulatto" means young mule. It was once believed that children with a Black parent and a white parent were like the mule, from two different species. While the word mulatto is still used today, it is not acceptable. I am not a mule. I am a whole person.

The official categories for race change depending on where you are in the world.

In the United States, there are five categories for race: White, American Indian or Alaska Native, Asian, Black or African American, and Native Hawaiian or other Pacific Islander. In South Africa, the racial categories are: Black African, Colored, Indian or Asian, White, and Other. ("Colored" refers to bi- and multiracial folx.) White, mestizo, and Black are the categories used in Uruguay. (Mestizo refers to folx who have European and Indigenous ancestry.)

In the United Kingdom, the categories for people are a mix of racial and ethnic identities. They include: White, Mixed/Multiple ethnic groups, Asian/Asian British, Black/African/Caribbean/Black British, and "Other" ethnic groups.

Seeing how every country has a different way of classifying people shows us that **RACE AND ETHNICITY REALLY ARE SOCIAL CONSTRUCTIONS.**

The words I use to describe my race have changed over

the years. My dad is Black and my mom is white. I have light brown skin, many freckles across my face, brown eyes, and curly hair. My ethnic identity encompasses all I know about our family background: English, African American, French, Irish, and (I've been told) Sioux. When I was a kid, our school district labeled us as white. Maybe because I lived with my white mom? Maybe because of my light skin? Maybe to fill some statistical quota? I don't know. I am Black biracial.[4]

Race is confusing. There is, of course, no scientific evidence that proves folx with the lightest skin are smarter, prettier, and better. But this has been the way we, as a species, have been doing things for centuries. Ta-Nehisi Coates writes in *Between the World and Me*:

We have been taught to categorize people based on their skin color, their nation of origin, and their physical features by the people with the most power. People in the dominant culture have worked for centuries to create laws, policies, and institutions to guarantee that they will always maintain that power. We'll look more closely at this in the next chapters.

Pull out your notebook or a piece of paper, grab a favorite pen, and find a place where you can think without interruption.

Take a deep breath and reflect on **your own race and ethnicity**. You may use these questions for guidance:

1. What do you know about your ethnic identity?
2. Is this something you and your family and friends have talked about?
3. Do you think about your race? (and how often?)
4. Do you think about your ethnic identity, too?
5. Do you feel like your racial identity and your ethnic identity are similar? Are they in harmony?

TAKE A DEEP BREATH.

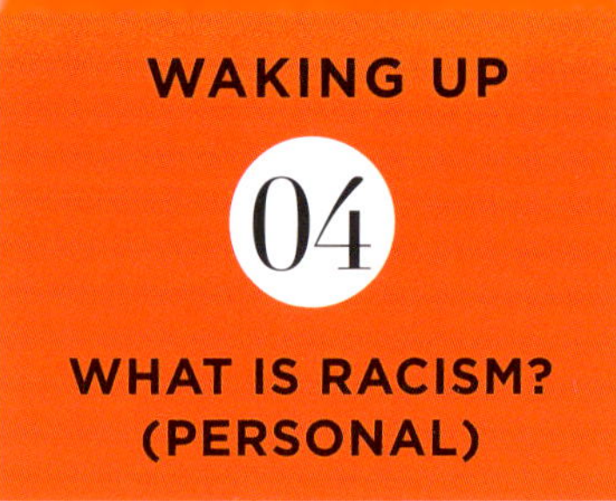

WAKING UP

04

WHAT IS RACISM? (PERSONAL)

Someone described racism to me as the smog we breathe. It is all around us; racism is everywhere. Our lives are polluted with racism and it harms us all. The more we are aware of this smog of racism, the better equipped we can become to combat this toxic way of being.

When folx hear the word racism, many different things come up because there are multiple different explanations and interpretations. Everyone has their own understanding and beliefs around racism. Some of the ones you may be most familiar with are:

RACISM IS A SYSTEM OF ADVANTAGES AND DISADVANTAGES BASED ON RACE.

PREJUDICE + POWER = RACISM

THE BELIEF THAT MEMBERS OF EACH RACE HAVE DIFFERENT CHARACTERISTICS. BECAUSE OF THIS, FOLX BELIEVE THAT SOME ARE **INFERIOR** AND SOME ARE **SUPERIOR**.

IT IS PREJUDICE OR DISCRIMINATION AGAINST SOMEONE BASED ON RACE.

The best definition I've ever heard came from an anti-racist training I did several years ago. Racism is personal prejudice and bias AND the **systemic** misuse and abuse of power by institutions. When I refer to racism, this is the definition I am using.

RACISM IS PERSONAL
PREJUDICE AND BIAS
AND THE SYSTEMIC MISUSE
AND ABUSE OF POWER
BY INSTITUTIONS

AFRO
AFRO
AFRO

Using this understanding of racism allows us to see how it truly impacts all of our lives. We have a lot of work ahead of us to break it down.

RACISM IS NOT JUST PREJUDICE!

Everyone has prejudices or **biases**. These are our judgments: the things we discriminate against. Some of our prejudices are conscious and some are not. They are things we've learned and assumed from everything around us. This includes the **stereotypes** we've witnessed. Whether you are in the dominant culture or not also contributes to your prejudices. We begin to form prejudices when we are two years old.[5] Our biases are absorbed, we take them in, and they become a part of our belief system. But they can change.

BEAUTY

In many places in the world people have absorbed the bias that light skin and European features are the most desirable. White people are considered to be the standard for beauty. (Does this sound familiar? We can thank Linnaeus and Blumenbach for this.) For hundreds of years people have believed and passed on the belief that folx with darker skin are inferior. Those with the lightest skin have been treated the best, have had the most power, and continue to pass along the bias that light skin is superior. To be considered beautiful, to fit into the box of what is considered "normal," some folx try to lighten their skin with bleaching creams and some use chemicals to alter their hair.

I spent several of my young teen years trying to force my naturally curly hair into straight "white" hair.

This cost my mom a lot of money, I wasted a lot of time sitting in the salon chair, and it caused a lot of pain on my head. The beautician placed a series of chemicals on my scalp to rearrange my curls, to undo the natural texture, and then, after several hours, straightened my hair with a very hot iron. This effect did not last very long. After about six weeks my hair started to grow and my kinky roots showed. The process of trying to not have curls caused burns on my scalp (which took weeks to heal) and my hair to break in large chunks. I kept this going until I was 15, when the kid whose locker was next to mine saw my curls after swimming. He said "Why don't you keep your hair like that?" I didn't have a good answer for him, or for myself. I kept my natural curls after that. My prejudice against my own curly hair and my desire to look more like my white friends caused me to dislike a part of myself.

We have been conditioned to the bias of whiteness. We can undo this. People play a big role in keeping racism going. If we do not work to recognize our prejudices, we remain a part of the problem. When we become aware of our biases and our role in racism, then we can begin to understand how we are a part of a system that is much bigger than us.

RACISM IS A PART OF OUR SOCIETY, BUT IT DOESN'T HAVE TO BE.

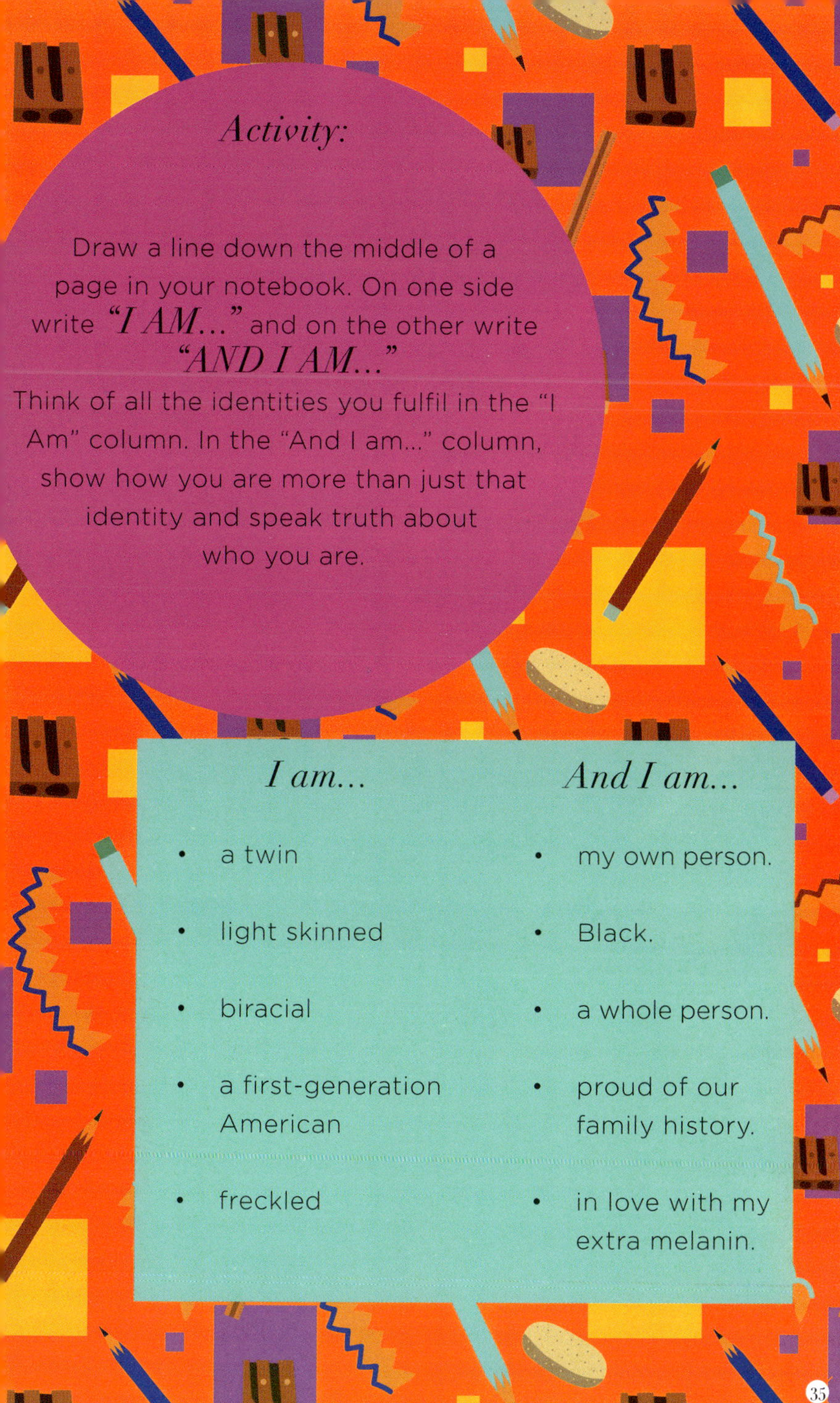

Activity:

Draw a line down the middle of a page in your notebook. On one side write *"I AM..."* and on the other write *"AND I AM..."*

Think of all the identities you fulfil in the "I Am" column. In the "And I am..." column, show how you are more than just that identity and speak truth about who you are.

I am...	*And I am...*
• a twin	• my own person.
• light skinned	• Black.
• biracial	• a whole person.
• a first-generation American	• proud of our family history.
• freckled	• in love with my extra melanin.

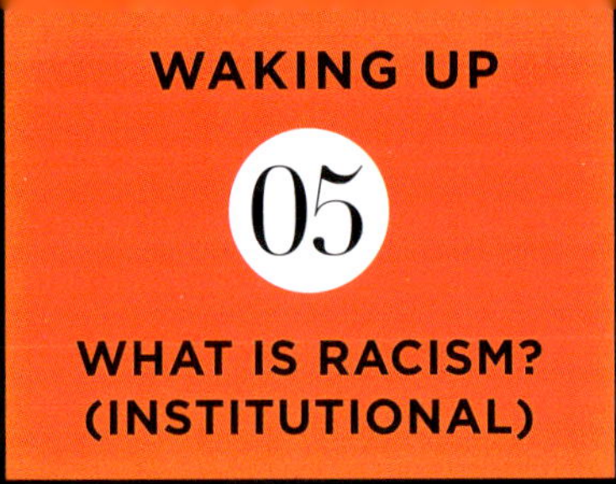

WAKING UP

05

WHAT IS RACISM? (INSTITUTIONAL)

What we do not know, our lack of information and knowledge, contributes to our prejudices and biases.

Many people, moments, and movements have been left out of history. The stories have almost always been told by those in the dominant culture. When you don't see Black and Brown folx on TV and in movies, when their stories are not in our history books, you begin to draw your own conclusions about why you regularly see white actors, authors, and models. This becomes your normal and it's easy to go along with this ordinary way of life.

WE MAKE ASSUMPTIONS BASED ON WHAT WE DO NOT SEE OR KNOW.

When you only read one account of history through a single lens, you do not have the whole truth.

In school we learned about local history, in Syracuse, New York. It's a midsize city on the land that once belonged to the Haudenosaunee people. We learned about the different tribes that made up the Confederacy and about the Onondagas who lived in longhouses and cultivated that land on what is now called Syracuse. Our teachers taught us little about the Onondagas. We learned about how they lived a long time ago, about Hiawatha, and wampum. We learned about the Haudenosaunee people in the past tense. Our teachers never invited anyone from the Onondaga Nation to speak to our classroom, never showed us pictures, or read us stories and articles from local Indigenous authors, artists, and activists. Because of that we, like many students in the United States, believed Native Americans only existed in history.

If stories of resistance and accomplishments are purposefully left out of our history books or told from the perspective of those in the dominant culture, we have no voice. No one knows who we are and that we exist. The legacy we are left with is one that has been shaped by the oppressors.

The Black Panther Party created the Free Breakfast for Children program, which is present in so many American neighborhoods and schools. But we may only know the Black Panther party from the biased headlines from newspapers. You may only see photos of them being arrested

STRICT BUSINESS RULES

STRUCTURAL RACISM

ONE KIND OF LOVE
SYSTEMATIC RACISM

and build your own conclusions that they were violent. Knowing who the members of the Black Panther Party are, their goals for their people, and learning about their resistance lets us be better stewards of the truth. If I hadn't heard their own words, I would never have known.

WHAT ARE INSTITUTIONS?

Examples of institutions are: the government, media and entertainment, business, housing, banks, the criminal justice system, education, and health care. Institutions create laws, policies, programs, and rules. People make up these institutions. Together, people and our institutions create a solid structure of racism through policies, rules, and opportunities that give more resources to one group than another. Here are some examples

Business

Although **discrimination** in the workplace is illegal, it continues to happen. According to recent studies, on average, 24% of **BIPoC** have experienced racial discrimination at work across Europe.[6] (This number climbs to 44% in Italy.) Discrimination based on skin color, physical appearance, accent, and country of birth were all reasons cited by respondents to the study.

In the US, businesses and corporations are allowed to have dresscodes, which can include very strict rules about the type of clothes you are allowed to wear, whether you can have visible tattoos and piercings, and how you wear your hair. Employers can create guidelines around "neutral hairstyles" and if a person is not able to adhere to these, they can be asked to leave or be fired. Businesses are supposed to respect racial differences under the Civil Rights Act; however, they can have policies that specifically say what types of hairstyles are not allowed. It is still legal for employers to ban dreadlocks.

(This is an anti-Black policy.) And until 2018, the US Navy banned dreadlocks, braids, and topknot buns, which are all styles often worn by Black nonbinary **femmes** and women. In the UK, businesses and corporations can set any dresscodes they like, whether they are respectful to racial differences or not.

Housing

The richest borough in London, UK—Kensington & Chelsea—is also where you'll find the greatest income inequality among the city's residents. Homes are the most expensive in this borough and some of the only affordable housing for working-class poor folx was in the 24-story Grenfell Tower public-housing complex. While people living just a block away were able to afford clean, safe, reliable housing, the residents of Grenfell were repeatedly ignored when they complained about poor living conditions and the cheap materials used for the building's upkeep. No one took the residents' complaints seriously. On June 14, 2017, a fire broke out in an apartment on the fourth floor. It was caused by a faulty freezer. Residents did not hear fire alarms because there were none. The 350 folx living in the 127 apartments were encouraged to "stay put" unless there was a fire inside their home. As the tower became quickly engulfed in flames, many residents were trapped and 72 folx (mostly BIPoC and those living close to and in poverty)[7] died. London mayor Sadiq Khan has criticized the government's response to the tragedy.[8] Lawyer Imran Khan QC has also said investigations failed to consider institutional racism in the safety breaches.[9] Discrimination in housing isn't solely an issue in the UK. It is a global issue. In the city of Philadelphia, USA, Black folx are three times less likely than their white counterparts to receive a loan.[10] While 69% of white people own homes, only 44% of Black folx do and, for over a decade, Black home ownership has been on the decline.[11] Flint, Michigan, has one of the highest proportions of BIPoC residents (with 57% being Black/African American) in the US. There, folx have not had a clean, safe water supply to drink since April 2014.[12] Michigan's mayor has said "race and class" were factors for this [continued] slow response to getting clean drinking water into the homes of Flint.[13]

Government and Justice

In South Africa, the government in 1948 was the Nationalist Party, which was made up of white colonialists. This government enacted the system of apartheid from 1948 to the 1990s. Apartheid was legalized racism and its purpose was to keep people segregated based on their race and to keep the white people with power in power. Later on, in chapter 8, you'll read more about Stephen Lawrence and how the UK criminal justice system misused their power. It took 19 years to find Stephen's killers guilty and, even then, only two of the five folx who were involved in the attack were convicted. After an inquiry into the London Metropolitan Police force, the results found the police department to uphold "institutional racism."[14]

Education

Less than 20% of teachers in the United States' public schools are Folx of the Global Majority, while over 50% of their student population are.[15] Teachers are more likely to send Black and Brown students to detention for being "disrespectful."[16] This is supported by rules that won't let students wear natural hairstyles, curriculums that don't reflect our cultures, and a teaching force that is predominantly white. Black, Asian, Indigenous, biracial and multiracial children are twice as likely as their white classmates to be referred to law enforcement from their schools or even arrested at their schools. Students can be arrested for "disorderly conduct," which can be anything from repeatedly speaking out in class, and not handing in your phone, to getting into a physical fight with another student – anything that can disrupt the "normal" teaching day. In the UK, only 1.5% of Cambridge and 1.2% of Oxford University first year students were Folx of the Global Majority in 2017.[17] While this percentage is much higher in the US, Black and Latinx folx are still represented less than white students.[18]

Health Care

There is a long history of racism in medicine in the UK/US: from the unethical, forced experimentation on enslaved folx, to immigrants being denied healthcare due to lack of citzenship.[19] Personal biases held by doctors and the historical oppression of Black, Brown, and Indigenous folx have not only led to a deep mistrust of medical professionals, but also to a lower life expectancy for BIPoC.[20] Around 4% of doctors in the US are Black and about 6% of doctors are Latinx.[21] White and non-Black doctors are more likely to hold anti-Black biases, which affect the way they treat patients.[22] Studies find that one of the biases held is believing Black folx have a higher tolerance for pain, which results in doctors not believing them when they seek help.[23] BIPoC experience unequal treatment to white patients who experience the same ailments, and doctors tend to lecture BIPoC and not respectfully communicate to them.[24,25] This leads to a sense of **internalized** inferiority in patients, who are less likely to seek the support of medical professionals. Without training to notice biases and address them, Folx of the Global Majority will continue to have a lower life expectancy.

Remember: institutions rely on people to maintain or change racism.

Activity:

NOTICE WHO HAS **POWER**:

Who is the head of your school?

Who is the president or prime minister of your country?

Who runs the biggest corporations?

Who teaches you?

Who are the authors you're reading?

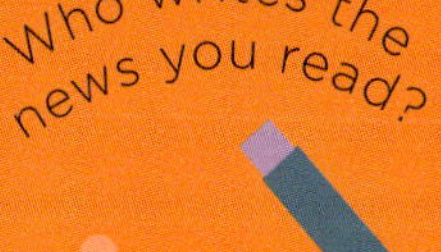

Who writes the news you read?

Who are the celebrities you see often (in magazines and the news?)

WHAT IS THE RACE OF EACH OF THESE FOLX?

DO THEY REFLECT THE DOMINANT CULTURE?

DO THESE FOLX FIT NEATLY INTO THE IMAGINARY BOX?

IF THEY DO NOT, DO THEY UPHOLD IDEAS THAT FIT INTO THAT BOX?

IN THIS SECTION:
• PREJUDICE IS PERSONAL
• THE HISTORY WE CARRY
• KNOWING OUR HISTORY
• WE ARE OUR HISTORY

OPENING THE WINDOW
MAKING SENSE OF THE WORLD

OPENING THE WINDOW

06

PREJUDICE IS PERSONAL

Can I share a story from my childhood with you? When I was at school, I had a teacher who liked to tell us about all the fun field trips and activities her two blond sons got to do at their school. We did not get to do those kinds of activities. They lived in the suburbs of our city. Their school had a lot more money than ours did. It also had teachers who cared about their students because their students were like them. I do not think my teacher cared about us, mostly Black and Brown children. As a white woman who existed mostly in the dominant culture, she shared her biases with us whether her intention was to do so or not.

The classroom appeared welcoming. Our desks were in small groups of four. The windows let in a lot of natural light. The reading corner in the back of the classroom was inviting with the orange chairs in a semicircle around the small rug. Our teacher read aloud to us every day. *My Teacher Is an Alien* was my most favorite.

But she did little things to remind us that she was in charge, that we were powerless, and that some of our lives were worth more and some of our lives were worth less.

One time, she refused to let my classmate use the restroom all morning long. His desk was diagonal from mine. He raised his hand (again). Our teacher ignored him until he had an accident that pooled at his feet and our desks. She wasn't empathetic or sympathetic. She yelled at him. He was the only Latinx boy in our classroom. He had done nothing wrong.

She tried to humiliate him and showed us all that she had the power to take away our humanity. She decided whether we could use the bathroom, not us. Her actions and words made my classmate feel so small. She showed us that she didn't care about us.

There was the other time she yelled at my darker friend in front of the classroom because he corrected her on the misinformation she gave us. He and I often corrected our teacher on her misspellings. I remember pointing out to her once that Asia should only have two *a's* instead of three. She yelled at him, called him the name of an animal, and prefaced it with "Black" and "African." She said those words with so much anger, they turned ugly in her mouth.

She tried to make us fear my friend. Her words told us there was something wrong with being Black and African. She tried to make us feel like he was less than human. She showed us she didn't care about us.

My teacher's prejudice was overt. And she had power. It was easy to see, hear, and feel. We could name it. She didn't like Black and Brown children. She didn't like our city school. That was obvious to us. We didn't understand why she was our teacher. Why did she stay at our school? Why was she allowed to stay there? Why did none of the other adults care that she was so unkind and unjust towards us, nine- and ten-year olds? I felt powerless in her classroom because she shared her racist beliefs with us every day in a very negative way. (I'll share with you some things you can do if you're in a situation like this in the next section!)

While some forms of racism are easy to notice and name, others are less overt. You may not be as aware of them right away.

For instance, for as long as I can remember, people (in particular, white people), have asked me, *"WHAT ARE YOU?"* Sometimes it's followed with, *"NO, LIKE, WHAT ARE YOU?"* Throughout my life I've answered differently. I am Tiffany. I am human. I am a person. I am Black. I am biracial. When I was a kid I never knew how to answer because I didn't know why I was being asked that question. Asking me what I am is a common microaggression that

folx in the dominant culture ask those in the subordinate culture. Because my race was not clear to some, they felt the need to question me in order to categorize me. They needed to know if I was "one of them" or not. I even had a friend make a game of guessing what my race is. Race isn't a game though; it's a part of our lives.

MICROAGGRESSION

A microaggression is an intentional or unintentional insult, slight, or hostile, negative message to folx who do not fit into the imaginary box of dominant culture. They can occur anytime and anywhere. Sometimes microaggressions are spoken, like someone saying, *"WHERE WERE YOU BORN?"* to an Asian British person in London.

Other times they are acted out, like crossing to the other side of the street when you see a Black man, or a shop owner ignoring a Brown person and only addressing the white customers. Microaggressions, no matter how small they may seem, are harmful.

INTERNALIZED RACISM

When you experience microaggressions repeatedly, the effects accumulate and can lead to low self-esteem, depression, poor health, and thinking the stereotypes are true. Believing that you are inferior, acting on the negative messages about folx of the same race as you, and even denying your ethnic and cultural heritage are examples of internalized racism.

PERSONAL RACISM

Personal racism reinforces the power of the institutions and the institutions uphold prejudice with racist laws and policies. Personal prejudice and acting on it is what killed Trayvon Martin in 2012. George Zimmerman used his fear of

Black men and his internalized racial superiority to justify why he felt "threatened" by the teenager. Trayvon was on his way to his dad's house from the convenience store. He carried a pack of Skittles and a can of iced tea in his hands. Zimmerman saw a stereotype and took Trayvon's life. Even as a grown man, he managed to see young Trayvon as a threat (He wasn't.) He was found not guilty of the murder because institutions created the tools to allow for him to go free. The **"Stand Your Ground law"** allowed for George Zimmerman to not be arrested after he shot and killed Trayvon Martin.[26] He claimed self defense (even though Zimmerman was in his car and Trayvon was walking to his dad's house) and, in Florida, if you use this claim, you may be exempt from being arrested. Understanding the ways racism lives in each of us allows us to ask questions and examine structures. Whether we hold on to internalized racial oppression (if you are a Person of the Global Majority) or internalized racial superiority (if you are white or a white-passing Person of Color), we need to be aware of the biases we hold and question them.

Activity:

Grab your notebook. Carry it around with you for a day, or longer.

Look and listen for the **microaggressions** around you.

Write them down and note your observations.

Notice who they are directed toward and who is saying and doing them.

Come back to these observations another day. Reflect on how these words and actions affect the person or group they are directed toward.

PREJUDICE

Before we move on, check you understand this term.
PREJUDICE
is the personal side of racism. It is in an attitude towards an individual or group of folx based on the social group they belong to. Prejudices can be based on stereotypes, misinformation, or fear, and—while they are not always negative—they most often are.

"WE CARRY OUR HISTORY WITH US. WE ARE OUR HISTORY."—JAMES BALDWIN

If we carry our history with us, what is it that we are carrying?

For me, it's living in the south side of Syracuse, New York, with my mom and sister. It's listening to Tina Turner in my dad's car. It's having milky tea with a square of Cadbury chocolate waiting for me after school at our nana and pop-pop's house. It's not crying at my grandfather's funeral. It's having the same textbooks my mom and uncles had when they were in school. It's not knowing my cousins on my dad's side of the family and forgetting what my uncles and aunts look like. It's walking home from the library with a heavy load of books. It's walking home from school without an adult for the first time. It's ice skating after school. It's staying late to work on choreography for the school musical. It's reading *The Autobiography of Malcolm X* on my own after my professor swapped it out for the movie *Thelma and Louise*. It's being the only one in my college classes. It's all of that and everything else.

IT'S SO MANY THINGS WITHIN ME. AND MY HISTORY IS MORE THAN JUST ME.

MY HISTORY BEGINS WITH ME

My history begins before me. It's between France and England when my family's name changed and became Anglicized. It's my mom moving across the ocean in a great big boat from England to New York. And, it's her losing her accent in school. It's my dad being drafted for the Vietnam War. And it's him lying in a hospital, in a coma, after driving while intoxicated. It's my pop-pop proposing to my nana. It's not knowing where the "Jewell" of my last name comes from.

My history begins before me. It begins before the stories I know and the ones I long to know. My history begins hundreds and hundreds of years ago... and so does yours.

WHAT IS THIS HISTORY WE CARRY WITH US?

The history we carry is the three servants, John Gregory, Victor (no surname), and John Punch, who escaped in 1640. The first two were white Europeans, and John Punch was a Black man from Africa. The three servants were caught in Maryland and brought back to their master in Virginia. All men were punished with 30 lashes. The two Europeans had one year added on to their servitude. But John Punch was sentenced to serving his master for the rest of his life. In the court ruling, the only thing that separated their sentences was their race. "And that the third being a negro named John Punch shall serve his said master ... for the time of his natural life here or elsewhere." John Punch was one of the first servants to be sentenced to slavery because of race.

COLONIZATION

The history we carry with us is of the **colonizer** and the colonized. Colonization is when a group with power and resources dominates another group, often by violence and manipulation. The land they control gives the colonizer even more power in the world. The people in colonized places become subjects under the rule of the dominant country.

The British colonized many people and places around the world at various times, including India, Jamaica, Somalia, Ghana, the United States, Burma, Canada, the Falkland Islands, Pakistan, South Africa, Zimbabwe, Egypt, Bahrain, Qatar, Australia, Singapore, Hong Kong, Malta, New Zealand and many more. They established settlements on Indigenous lands, took and used resources, and exploited the people of that country. And Britain was not the only colonizer.

Denmark controlled Greenland and parts of Ghana. France colonized Haiti, Chad, the Republic of Congo, Mali, Senegal, Cambodia, Laos, Vietnam, and many other places. Spain dominated the Philippines and Guam, Costa Rica, El Salvador, Paraguay, and Colombia, among other places. The list goes on.

In France, the history we carry with us is Louis XIV setting up *Le Code Noir* (the Black Code) in 1685, establishing laws that inhibited enslaved Black folx (specifically) from having any rights. They were declared as "movable," which means they could be bought and sold and passed down from generation to generation. They were not allowed to own anything. The enslaved Black person's testimony held no value in court and, while they could be convicted of a crime, if they were a victim of a crime, justice was not pursued. *Le Code Noir* ensured that slavery passed on from mother to children. This guaranteed that even those who were children of white masters and born to enslaved mothers did not have the same freedoms their fathers did.

White Europeans colonized much of the world where Indigenous, Black, and Brown folx had lived for many years. Colonization separated people from their families, their language, and their land. Colonial rule had a lasting impact that we are still recovering from and reconciling with today.

The environment has not been able to recover from the constant farming, building, and deforestation that began when civilizations continued to expand. People and their labor were exploited by the colonizers to strip the earth of resources: from gold, to salt, to diamonds, to oil.

And colonial rule never truly left. While some countries are sovereign, and are not officially owned by other nations, they were left without many of their natural resources, left with overly harvested land, and infertile earth.

A more recent relationship that has been created between the colonizer and the colonized is in the form of aid and charity. We now have people and countries who had their resources and wealth stolen from them and now need support to survive. This relationship can be labeled as white saviorism, in which well-intentioned people believe they can save folx who were stripped of their resources rather than giving back the power and giving up their privilege.

The transatlantic slave trade was catastrophic for Black African families and had a very lasting effect as we are still, centuries later, healing from the **ancestral trauma**. **Chattel slavery** used the made-up science that folx of different skin tones and from different geographical areas are biologically different and either superior or inferior to justify the enslavement of Black and Brown folx.

The legacy that was left for us is the **systematic** oppression of BIPoC folx. It's our schools being more segregated today than they were during the time of legal segregation. It's our communities being purposefully divided by city architects, with the support of government offices and banks. It's evidenced by the higher rate of Black folx being incarcerated than white people. It's left the median white family with 41 times more wealth than the median Black family.[27]

The legacy of enslavement has left us with racist attitudes being our everyday normal.

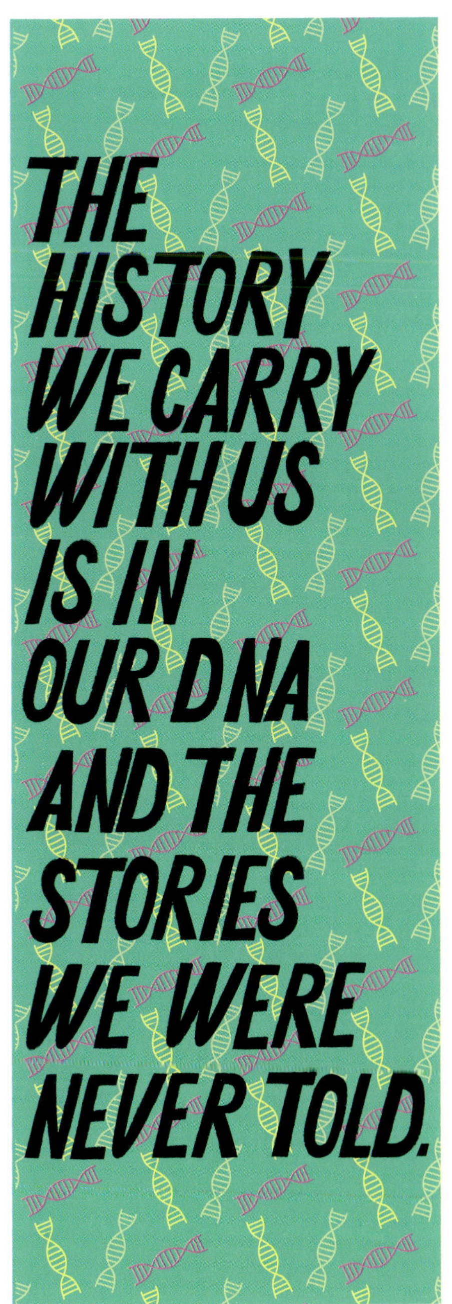

my history

Activity:

Pause for a moment. Give yourself some time to write out **your history**.

What is your history? Where are you from? What stories of your life have shaped you into who you are at this moment?

What is the history of your family? What are the stories you are always told? What are the stories you don't know enough about and would like to know more of?

Write your history!

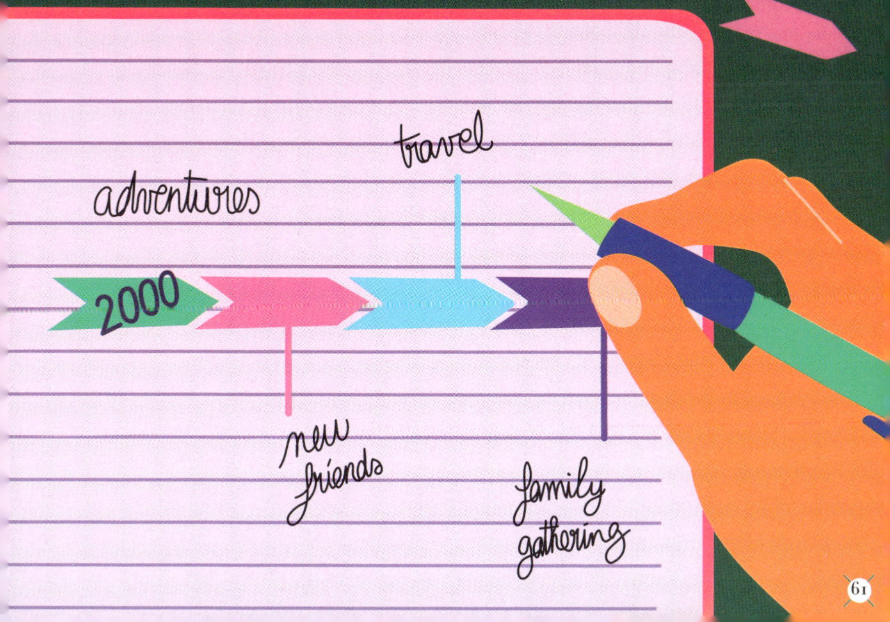

adventures

travel

2000

new friends

family gathering

OPENING THE WINDOW

08

KNOWING OUR HISTORY

Racism is everywhere and has been a part of our histories for hundreds and hundreds of years. And it carries on, around the world.

In America, the history we carry with us is the Indian boarding schools started in 1860. The goal was to **assimilate** Indigenous folx into the "American culture."

The government agency, the Bureau of Indian Affairs, established the first school on the Yakama Reservation. Children were taught the values of the dominant culture (and the Protestant religion) to become "civilized." The United States government had 60 schools where over 6,000 Indigenous youth were subjected to "learning" the ways of the white man. In 1893 a court ruling declared mandatory education for Indigenous youth. This was enforced by the police and government agents who took children from their families. When communities resisted (which they did), their food rations and resources, which were controlled by the government, were withheld.

Still, it was believed the schools needed to be off reservation land and away from tribal influence in order for children to be completely assimilated out of their culture. The Carlisle Indian School was established in 1879 by Colonel Richard Henry Pratt, who served as headmaster for 25 years. He is known for saying "Kill the Indian, save the man." [28] He believed in completely removing children from their families and homes on the reservations and keeping them fully immersed in white society in order to assimilate into the dominant culture. Female students spent more than half of the school day being trained to cook, clean, and sew, and male students were trained to be farmers, and blacksmiths. The conditions for many were inadequate. Food was withheld as punishment, children were used for local domestic labor, and they were forced to live far from their families and homes.

In 1978 Native American families were finally granted the right to choose the type of education their children received and were able to keep them on the reservation and with their families. **1978 WASN'T THAT LONG AGO.**

These schools were the model for the residential schools in Australia and New Zealand. In 1814 they were set up by Christian churches and funded by the British government. These schools were created to assimilate and train Indigenous, Aboriginal, and Maori children to do service jobs. The last residential schools were finally closed down in the 1980s. The children who were forced to attend these schools are known as the **"stolen generation."**

Education was used as a weapon, taking Indigenous children from their families and stripping them of their hair, language, culture and heritage, and their names.

The history we carry with us is the Windrush generation. The children of the colonized traveled from the Caribbean Commonwealth to Britain on a big ship called the *HMT Empire Windrush*. Thousands of folx came to the UK from colonized countries from 1948 to 1971. They came from Jamaica, Barbados, Trinidad and Tobago, and several other Caribbean countries to work. The British government invited them because there was a shortage of labor in the years after World War Two. The Immigration Act of 1971 stated all citizens of Commonwealth countries living in Britain were able to live in Britain for as long as they'd like (indefinitely). Many folx of the Windrush generation came to the country on their parents' passports. Many of them already thought themselves to have British citizenship and did not have their own paperwork and passports. Since January 1973, stricter laws around immigration have required folx to prove their continued residency in the UK. Employers, hospitals, landlords, and police were encouraged to check paperwork and prove folx did not belong in the country. Without that proof, this generation of people were threatened with deportation and the loss of national medical care and their jobs. These stricter laws were created to keep immigrants from coming to Britain and, in dong so, also managed to leave a generation of folx feeling unwelcome in their homes.[29]

The history we carry with us is in our schools. We still feel the effects of the *Brown v. Board of Education* court ruling today. The 1954 Supreme Court decision overturned the 1896 law that allowed schools, businesses, and institutions in the United States to have "separate, but equal" facilities for Black and white people. This felt like a big win for many. School integration began. Students like Linda Brown and, later, Ruby Bridges and the Little Rock Nine were some of the first Black youth to enter into white schools. Before this, they were in schools run by Black educators for Black children and families. The quality of the buildings and their materials were not equal to those that white children received.

As they entered into their new schools, Black students were met with harassment

and threats of violence from both white students and adults.

Many teachers did not want to teach Black and Brown students, and many white families did not want their children sitting alongside and learning with Black children. The court's decision was that Black children should have the same resources available to them as white children. But one of the results of this was the schools for Black children were closed and Black teachers lost their jobs. This resulted in Black children being left with all white teachers who held the belief that Black folx are inferior to white people. They did not understand their new students because they looked at them through a racist lens. We are still feeling the effects of this today with over 80% of the

teaching population being white while about half of the student population in the United States is comprised of Black, Brown, and Indigenous folx.[30]

In 1959 Prince Edward County in Virginia, choosing not to integrate its schools, closed down the whole school system for five years. Private schools were opened for white children in the county. These were supported by state taxes. Black children were denied an education because of the color of their skin. Five years is a long time.

The history we carry with us is the "collective failure" of how the London Metropolitan Police responded to the killing of 18-year-old Stephen Lawrence. On April 22, 1993, he was stabbed by a gang of white men in southeast London. Stephen was with his friend Duwayne Brooks, who was able to escape the attack. He helped the police identify the murderers (who were also named by an anonymous witness). The police arrested five white men weeks after Stephen was killed; however, in July, the charges were dropped because the authorities claimed Stephen's friend was not a reliable witness. 19 years after he was murdered, two of the suspects were found guilty of Stephen's murder. During those 19 years, Stephen's family opened up an architecture center in honor of Stephen; the suspects of his murder were jailed for a racist attack on an off-duty cop and, later, for distributing drugs, and the Metropolitan Police underwent a review led by Sir William Macpherson.

The results of the Macpherson Report led to over 70 recommendations on how to have "zero tolerance" for racism. Some of the suggestions were to change laws, improve the attitudes

RESISTANCE IS IN OUR HISTORY TOO.
BLACK LIVES MATTER

of the mostly white police force, and recruit and retain police that represent the population of folx they serve. Macpherson wrote that the police's response to Stephen Lawrence's killing was "institutionally racist." While some changes have been implemented, Black folx are still eight times more likely to be stopped by police than white people, and about one-fifth of the Metropolitan Police's 2,000 police officers and staff has an ethnicity bias that impacts their behavior. Stephen is now honored every April 22nd in a national commemoration of his life. Stephen Lawrence should still be alive today.

The history we carry with us is the police bombing of the Black liberation group,MOVE in a West Philadelphia neighborhood in 1985. It's the ban on wearing the full burqa in France, Denmark, Austria, Belgium, the Netherlands, and several other European countries. Here, racism, sexism, and Islamophobia meet at the intersections.

The history we carry with us includes those who died while in the custody and care of the United States Immigration and Customs Enforcement (ICE) Detention centers. Their names are: Roxana Hernández, Jakelin Caal Maquin, Felipe Alonzo-Gomez, Mariee Juárez, and quite a few others.

We carry it with us and this history is built into our bodies and memories. It affirms who we are and how we have been taught by society to be. Our histories are there and we have the power to share them and speak the truth. Looking through our collective history, we can see how each of these moments has led to building the solid foundation of racism. **However, there has always been the work of disruption.**

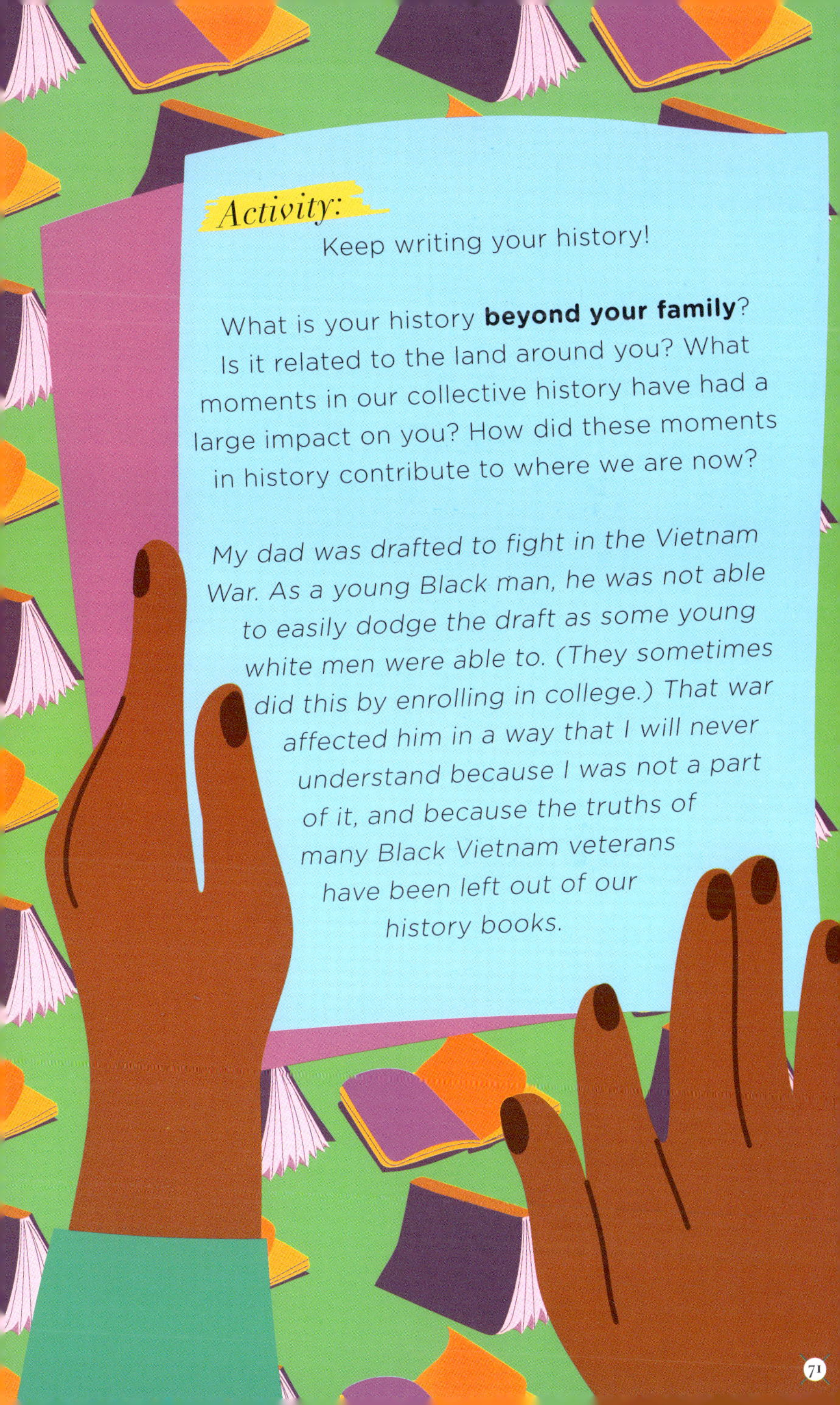

Activity:

Keep writing your history!

What is your history **beyond your family**? Is it related to the land around you? What moments in our collective history have had a large impact on you? How did these moments in history contribute to where we are now?

My dad was drafted to fight in the Vietnam War. As a young Black man, he was not able to easily dodge the draft as some young white men were able to. (They sometimes did this by enrolling in college.) That war affected him in a way that I will never understand because I was not a part of it, and because the truths of many Black Vietnam veterans have been left out of our history books.

1. Studio portrait of Esau Prescott, wearing boarding school uniform, Wisconsin, USA, 1915.

2. Sioux boys arrive at the Carlisle School, USA, 1879.

6. West Indian immigrants arrive at Victoria Station, UK, 1956.

5. Linda Brown outside Sumner Elementary School, Kansas, USA, 1953.

3. Jamaican immigrants arriving at Tilbury Docks in Essex, UK, 1948.

4. Education segregation in schools after white boycott, USA, 1964.

While some were working hard to build the foundation of racism into the solid structure it is today, there has always been resistance to racism. The stories of strength, of love, of joy, and of revolution are a part of our history too. Caribbean American poet and activist June Jordan wrote, **"WE ARE THE ONES WE HAVE BEEN WAITING FOR."**

WE HAVE ALWAYS BEEN AND WE WILL ALWAYS BE. THIS IS WHAT WE CARRY WITH US TOO.

Our history is Haiti, the first Black republic. From 1625 to November 18, 1803, France controlled the island of Saint-Domingue (now called Haiti). It was the most profitable French colony, producing goods from the labor of enslaved folx. In 1791, inspired by the "Declaration of the Rights of Man" and the 1789 Revolution in France, Toussaint Louverture (a former slave) led the rebellion against the white planters. The planters were the wealthiest people, who owned plantations, enslaved people, and controlled all the resources. Louverture believed in liberty and equality and one of his goals was to abolish slavery.

By 1792, Louverture and his army controlled a third of the island. In 1794 they expanded the revolution and moved the rebellion into Santo Domingo (now

JUNE
JORDAN

known as the Dominican Republic), where the Spanish had enslaved the Indigenous Taíno population as well as Africans and folx from other Caribbean countries.

In 1801 Toussaint Louverture declared himself the governor-general for life. Napoleon Bonaparte was the ruler of France at the time and he reinstated the Code Noir and, in hopes of restoring French rule and slavery in Saint-Domingue, sent thousands of troops to the island to capture Louverture and end the rebellion.

Toussaint Louverture and the French agreed to a truce, but that was broken and he was taken to France, where he died while in prison in 1803. Jean-Jacques Dessalines, a former slave and a general in Louverture's army, carried on the revolution and, on November 18, 1803, the French forces were defeated and withdrew from the island. On January 1, 1804 Dessalines declared the island an independent nation and named it Haiti, which means land of high mountains in Taíno. While Haiti has a long and complicated history, like all countries that were once colonized, we celebrate the stories of resistance and hope from our first Black republic.

Our history is with Yuri Kochiyama. After the bombing of Pearl Harbor (in Hawai'i) during World War Two, the US military was given the power to arrest, round up, detain, and intern any and all Japanese and Japanese-American people who resided on the West Coast. There were ten internment camps and about 120,000 folx were detained between 1942 and 1945. They lost their homes and businesses. Yuri Kochiyama was sent to an internment camp in Kansas. Kochiyama grew her strong activist roots while living in Harlem, New York. She worked in solidarity with Black activists and was close friends with

Malcolm X. She believed in Black liberation and understood how the misuse of institutional power kept all BIPoC oppressed. She also worked with the Young Lords Party advocating for Puerto Rican liberation. Yuri spent her life supporting political prisoners and was often the first person called to facilitate discussions with the police. She protested the Vietnam War and advocated reparations be made for the thousands of Japanese and Japanese Americans who were wrongfully detained during World War Two.

Yuri Kochiyama dedicated her life to resisting, raising consciousness, and working in solidarity for anti-racism and liberation. She passed away in 2014 and her words will remain with us always.

"TRANSFORM YOURSELF FIRST... BECAUSE YOU ARE YOUNG AND HAVE DREAMS AND WANT TO DO SOMETHING MEANINGFUL, THAT IN ITSELF, MAKES YOU OUR FUTURE AND OUR HOPE."

The history we carry with us is the Loving family. Richard Loving was white and Mildred Loving was Black Indigenous biracial. They were married in Washington, DC and living in Virginia (in 1958), where it was illegal to marry someone of a different race than you. (This was also illegal in over 20 other states in the US at the time.) They were woken one night by police entering into their home to arrest them. Richard and Mildred moved to Washington, DC; however, they missed their family and friends. After five years away from home Mildred sought support from the NAACP and the ACLU. The Lovings went to court in hopes of appealing the Virginia law, but the state wouldn't change. So the Lovings went to the highest court in the US, the Supreme Court. The court struck down the law in the *Loving v. Virginia* case, and marrying someone of a different race became legal in the US. Today, those of us who were born after the Loving case can call ourselves the "Loving Generation." I much prefer this to being called mixed. I am able to not only honor Mildred and Richard Loving when I refer to myself as a person of the Loving generation, I am also able to center love within my identity.

The history we carry with us is the League of Coloured Peoples, founded in Britain in 1931, by Dr. Harold Moody as an organization promoting civil rights, in response to not being able to find work as a qualified doctor.

Our history is with the activists and change-makers: Kwame Ture (formerly Stokely Carmichael), Marielle Franco, Fannie Lou Hamer, Dolores Huerta, Maya Angelou, Grace Lee Boggs, Steve Biko, Bayard Rustin, Quanah Parker, Gloria Anzaldúa, Claudette Colvin, Brittany Packnett, Alicia Garza, Patrisse Cullors, Opal Tometi, Marley Dias, and so many more.

WE CALL IT
LIBERATION.

THE HISTORY WE CARRY WITH US IS IN EACH AND EVERY ONE OF US. YOU WILL MAKE YOUR ANCESTORS PROUD. YOU ARE A PART OF THEIR STORIES OF RESISTANCE. YOU WILL MOVE US FORWARD.

Fannie Lou Hamer
Maya Angelou
Bayard Rustin
Marley Dias
Brittany Packnett
Grace Lee Boggs
Dolores Huerta
Claudette Colvin
Steve Biko

Activity:

And, still, there's more history to write. (You may soon have to get a new notebook!)

Are there stories in your family of how folx **resisted racism**? Of how they worked with others to fight unjust laws?

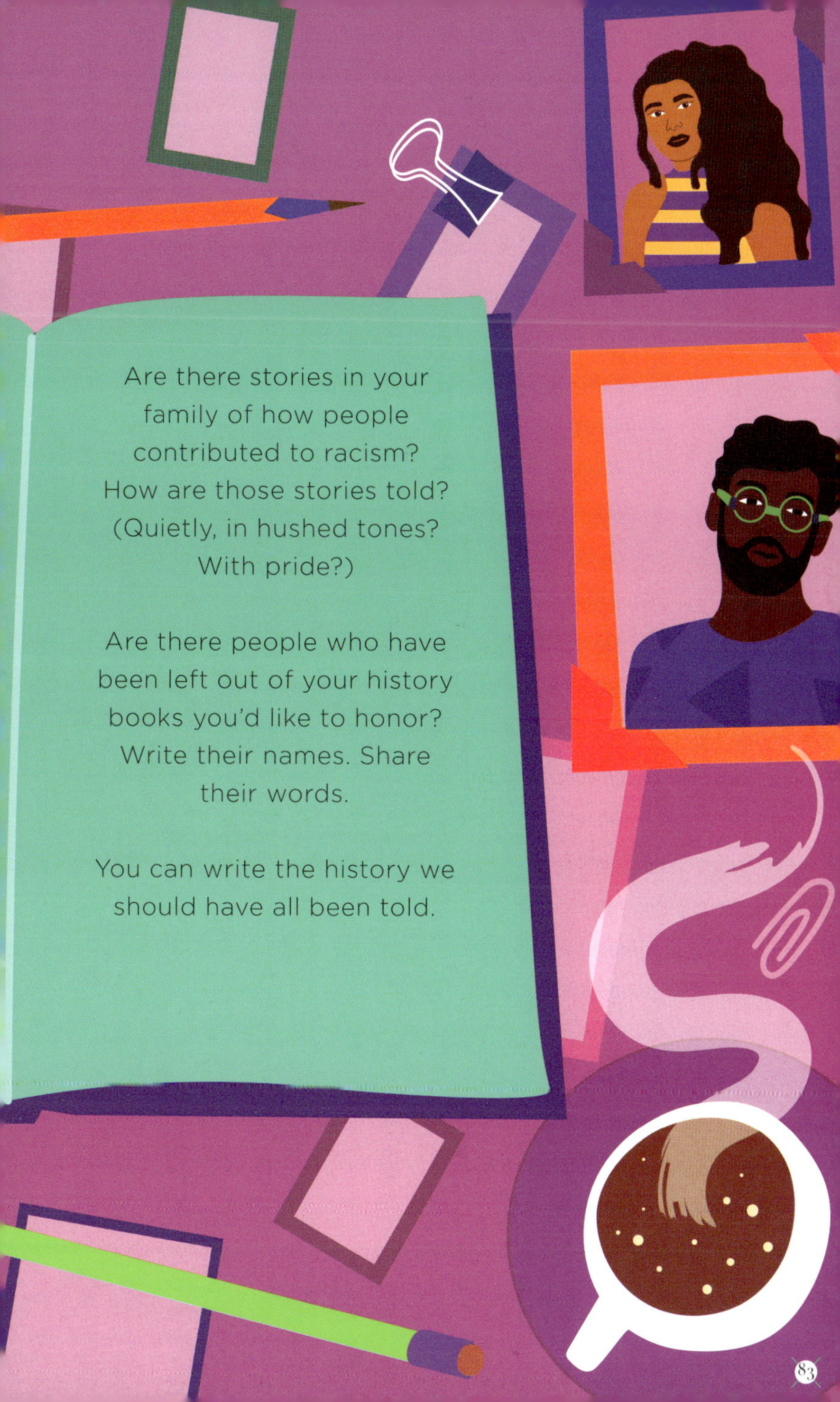

Are there stories in your family of how people contributed to racism? How are those stories told? (Quietly, in hushed tones? With pride?)

Are there people who have been left out of your history books you'd like to honor? Write their names. Share their words.

You can write the history we should have all been told.

IN THIS SECTION:
• DISRUPT!
• TAKE ACTION!
• INTERRUPT!
• SOLIDARITY
• CALLING IN AND CALLING OUT

CHOOSING MY PATH

TAKING ACTION AND RESPONDING TO RACISM

CHOOSING MY PATH 10

DISRUPT!

HOW DO I STAND UP? AND SPEAK OUT? WHAT HAPPENS IF I DON'T SAY ANYTHING?

YOU CAN DO IT. YOU CAN DISRUPT RACISM AND CHANGE THE "NORMAL."

You are now able to see the world in a way you didn't always notice before. You are building a new lens to see yourself and the world around you. You know more history (the parts you are told about and what has been left out). You are more conscious of the ways people interact with one another. You are attuned to microaggressions and are aware of their impact. You see the work institutions have put in over hundreds of years to maintain the structure of racism. Your school may have rules around how students can wear their hair or what folx can wear on their head and you understand how this is affirming the dominant culture. You notice that, still, most of the shows and movies you watch have a nearly all-white cast and how every time there is a terrorist that person is Western Asian and speaks Arabic. You see how stereotypes are created and sustained. You have the tools to seek out more knowledge and gain a deeper understanding.

What do you do next?

You have a voice. Use it. Speak the truth. Share it with others. Choosing silence is not an option. Audre Lorde, an American feminist, writer, and activist said,
"MY SILENCES HAD NOT PROTECTED ME. YOUR SILENCE WILL NOT PROTECT YOU."

YOU CANNOT HEAR SILENCE. INACTION CANNOT BE SEEN. WE CANNOT FEEL THE MOMENTUM OF CHANGE IF NOTHING HAPPENS.

Use your voice to speak the truth about injustice and share the history we are often not told. Talk to your family, your friends, your classmates, anyone and everyone who will listen. Write and write and write and share. Create art and share it. Take risks. You can do this.

I wish I had used my voice when my teacher was so continually awful to us. I wish I had stood up to my teacher. And to our school administration that allowed her to remain there.

What would I do today if I were in that classroom?

I'd physically stand up to her (in my small nine-year-old self). I'd get out of my seat, stand up, and tell her, "You can't talk to him like that. It's not okay."

Then, I'd walk out of that classroom, bringing my friend with me and anyone else who wanted and needed to come. I would walk down the stairs to the office, where I'd ask the school secretary or the principal to file a complaint against that teacher. I'd tell them what happened. I'd tell them she verbally abused my friend. And I'd file that complaint. I would ask the office to call my friend's parents. He shouldn't have to sit another minute in the classroom with our teacher who assaulted him with her racist words. No one should.

I'd tell my mom. (I did.) We'd talk to his parents. I'd ask all our classmates to share what happened with their families. Our parents and caregivers would help our voices to be heard. We would be louder than just my own voice. They, too, would file complaints and show up at school the next morning. They'd ask for the resignation of our teacher because she should not be teaching us if she couldn't keep us safe. And she couldn't keep us safe because she was the one causing the harm.

We would all attend the next school board meeting to demand our schools be a place where we can learn, free from racial violence, both verbal and physical.

I think about that day so often and wish I had had the tools to go beyond recognizing what was happening. I wish I had created a plan and spoken up. I wish I had resisted my teacher and everything that kept her in place.

THIS IS WHY I SHARE WITH YOU. YOU CAN RESIST NOW. YOU CAN DISRUPT NOW.

What if it's something beyond your daily interactions at school? What if it's something outside of the comfort of what is familiar?

What if you and your family or friends are driving through town, and you see four police officers surrounding two young Black men? Maybe you recognize them, maybe you don't. Maybe one of them was in chorus with you last year. Maybe you've seen them at the store. Or maybe you don't know them at all. It doesn't matter if you know them or not.

You may be able to see if the police are armed. You may not. (While some police carry guns and others do not, we do know that they all carry power in their role as law enforcement.) You can see the young Black men are not armed, that they look confused, and that their hands are up.

You've seen the news over and over again; you know history. You think of Eric Garner, Sandra Bland, Philando Castile, Michael Brown, and all the others. You know this happens every day and today can be the day you change that. Here is where you can make a plan so you'll know what you can do if this does come up in your life. **NOTE:** You must make sure YOU are safe and out of harm's way. Talk to a trusted adult BEFORE taking any action.

Activity:

First, grab your notebook. Let's start writing!

You've observed what's happening and have examined the situation. You know the folx being held by the police look frightened. They don't want to be there. You don't want these two young Black men to become new hashtags and statistics.

So, there are a bunch of things you can do—take a few minutes and make a list of **every possible outcome** you can think of.

Here's my list:

- Ask the person who is driving the car to stop. We get out and walk over to the situation so we can stand witness.

- Record what is happening with my phone. I can. This is my right to do so. In the United States, the UK, and many other countries I cannot get arrested for recording if I take photos or video of public spaces. The police cannot take my phone from me. (They need a warrant to do so.) They may ask me to stop recording, but I don't have to stop.

If I am inside a store, private property, etc. the owner sets the rules and it is their choice whether I can record or not. This is not the decision of the police.

- Stay in the car and record.

- Stay in the car and shout out to the two being held by the police, "I see this."

- Standing near the police and the young men, I can ask the two Black men if there's anything I can do... if there's anyone I can call for them. (The adults I'm with can stand with me too.)

- Stop other people walking by and ask them to stand witness too. (There is strength and power in numbers.)

- Ask the adult I'm with to intervene while I stay in the car.

- Ignore this and keep driving.

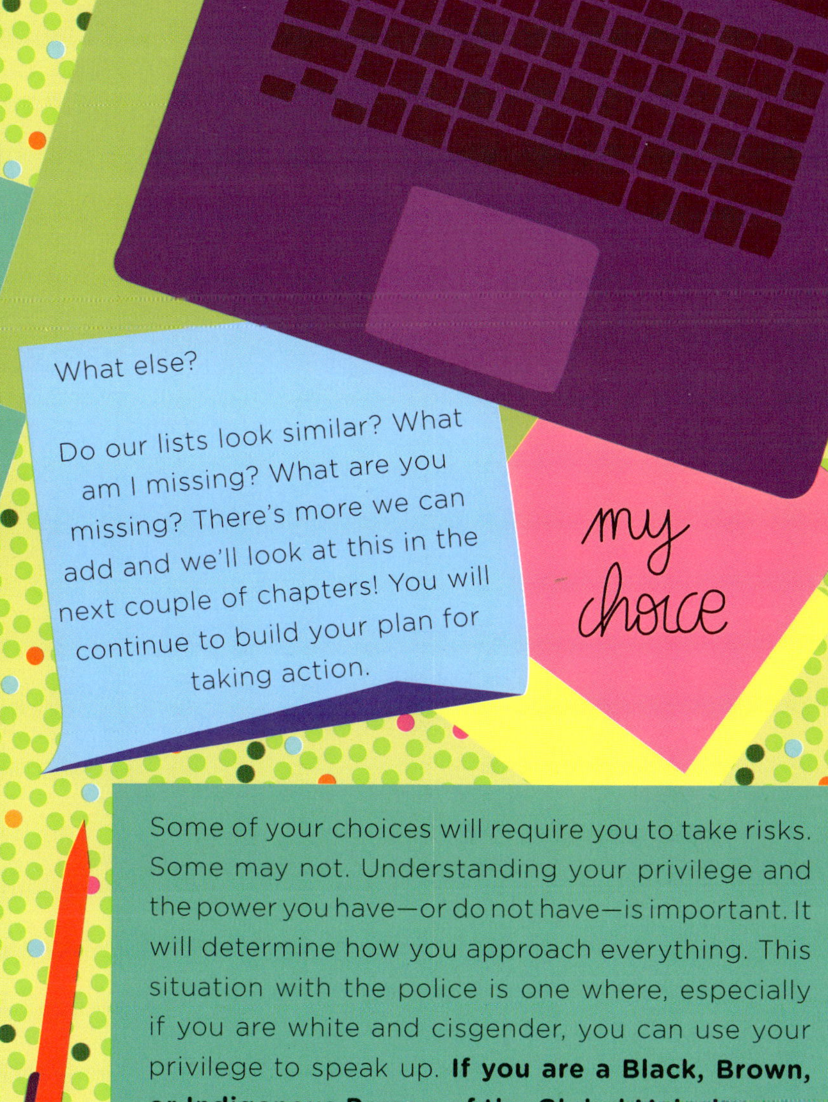

Some of your choices will require you to take risks. Some may not. Understanding your privilege and the power you have—or do not have—is important. It will determine how you approach everything. This situation with the police is one where, especially if you are white and cisgender, you can use your privilege to speak up. **If you are a Black, Brown, or Indigenous Person of the Global Majority, you will need to decide how each outcome could end for you**. White people, this is not something you need to do because you are at the center of the system: taking a risk with any of these choices will, most likely, not have you end up in jail or harmed.

CHOOSING MY PATH

11

TAKE ACTION!

WHAT HAPPENS IF I DON'T SAY ANYTHING? IF I DON'T TAKE ACTION? IF I DO NOTHING?

If you do nothing, everything stays the same. I didn't take action against my teacher and I had to sit in her classroom every day. That wasn't okay. She continued to make us feel small and powerless.

There are times you won't say anything. It may be because you don't see the injustice. Maybe you can't figure out what is happening and hope someone else will. Or maybe you can't do something because it's not safe. I didn't speak up because I didn't think I could. I was nine years old. I relied on the adults and thought they would speak up for us. They didn't.

DON'T WAIT TO SPEAK UP. DON'T WAIT TO TAKE ACTION.

When you are silent absolutely nothing changes. You are reinforcing the dominant culture. You are allowing racism to continue on. You not saying anything also tells others you are complicit (okay) with the status quo (how things are).

Being aware isn't enough. You must take action. You can do this in many different ways. It won't always be the

same for every situation because each situation is different. The thing we can count on is that racism exists. Here are some examples of ways I've taken action in my life.

When I was 11, taking action took the form of writing a poem and speaking out against our history lessons that glorified European colonialism and left out the truth. We didn't learn about who existed on the land until after Christopher Columbus turned up.

When I was in high school, I worked with a group that sold T-shirts and cards to raise funds to support the work of folx working with communities to build schools, toilets, maternity care, and gardens. My sister wrote for a local newspaper and shared her voice in the weekly insert for teens.

When I was 22, I helped to organize protests against predatory lenders (banks who give unfair loans) and an unjust health-care system. I worked in solidarity with Black and Latinx community members. Standing up against institutions that continually abuse their power to keep BIPoC oppressed deserves our attention and vigilance.

When I was 27, I used my voice to share the truth with my students, openly talking about power and privilege. We learned about the history of racism and resistance. We shared this with our families, school community, and other educators.

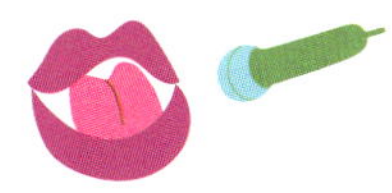

AND STILL, TODAY, EVERY DAY IT LOOKS DIFFERENT.

I am always working to understand who I am. What does it mean for me to be a light biracial Black cis female? Action takes the form of being aware and noticing injustice and checking stereotypes. It's using my lens of anti-racism, figuring out what it is I'm seeing, and taking action.

Remaining silent is not okay. It is not an option. Black folx, Brown folx, Indigenous folx, and Folx of the Global Majority are being harmed, oppressed, and killed every day. If you are white, light (like me), or a non-Black Person of the Global Majority, use your privilege and your proximity (or closeness) to the center of the dominant culture box to fracture the very foundation of our racist society. If you keep doing this and continue to put more cracks and dents into the structure, you'll shake it all up so it can crumble.

Activity 1:

Take a moment to pause and check in with yourself.
What action are you comfortable taking? What have you done?
What do you feel like you can do?
What action are you willing to do that goes beyond your comfort level?
What do you need in order to lean into your discomfort with these actions? What kind of support? (And from whom?)

Activity 2:

Imagine you have an anti-racist toolbox that you carry around with you. What's in it and why?

Here are some of the things I have in mine:

- A notebook and a pen so I can write down observations, thoughts, etc.
- Photographs of my family and friends to help ground me and keep me connected with those who I trust and love.
- Chocolate and almonds for quick energy.
- A reusable water bottle because I need to stay hydrated.
- Tiger Balm is in there. When I get stressed the tension builds in my shoulders and neck. It hurts. The Tiger Balm helps to ease that pain.
- I always have a book or two to read and make sure they're by BIPoC authors and folx living outside the imaginary box.
- Information about my rights in English and Spanish.
- My phone (charged) so I can easily connect with others and take photos and videos.

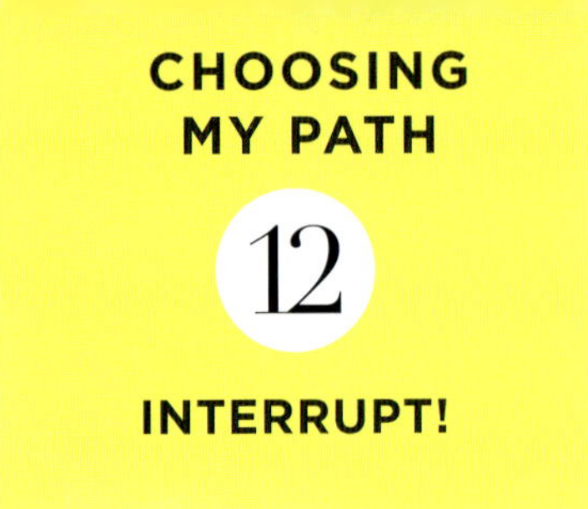

CHOOSING MY PATH

12

INTERRUPT!

Having more information, new knowledge, and facts, as opposed to the whitewashed stories of history, is a good start. It's just a start though. You are no longer a person who adheres to the center of the imaginary box. You have the great capacity to think. This is one of your superpowers. You are able to problem solve and make decisions. You have the power of choice.

You are able to pause and reflect. So, let's do that for a moment.

Grab your notebook and your favorite writing implement. (I like to use a fast-drying ink pen with three colors. I usually write in blue, but like that I can have an immediate choice.)

Activity:

WHAT ARE YOUR SUPERPOWERS?

Spend a couple minutes making a list of your superamazing powers. Not the ones you want to have. Not the ones someone else told you that you have. These are the superpowers you have that others may not even recognize. Here's what I wrote down: dancing, baking bread, reading, spelling, interrupting people to interject my opinions, sharing information, finding things. Now let's explore two of these in detail.

SUPER POWERS

FINDING THINGS OTHER PEOPLE LOSE

MAKING LISTS

SHARING NEW INFORMATION I'VE LEARNED WITH OTHERS

INTERRUPTING PEOPLE TO INTERJECT MY OPINIONS AND THOUGHTS INTO THE CONVERSATION

SPELLING

SUPERPOWER 1: INTERRUPTION

Many people around me will probably disagree with me when I share that one of my superpowers is to interrupt others so I can share what's on my mind. They would probably tell you it's annoying, rude, or frustrating. And, I'm sure it is to them. But, here's the thing about this superpower of mine: it is really quite useful. I have to be mindful of how to use it. If I never use this superpower, when it comes time to use my skills of interruption, it may not work because I'm out of practice or folx won't be used to hearing my voice. And if I constantly interrupt, there's the chance no one will listen, that I'll be ignored.

I practice this superpower when I'm in meetings with other adults. It's a really good time to do that because, often, the other adults I'm with will say something that's worth interrupting. If I hear someone share a stereotype or microaggression, I interrupt them!

Here's an example:

I'm meeting with a bunch of other teachers and hear someone say, **"Well, I don't see color. Race isn't really an issue in my classroom."** I could just ignore them but, because I know that's a microaggression AND because my superpower is interrupting, I can take action.

I can go ahead and interject. I don't need to wait for them to finish their monologue. I shouldn't let them go on because other folx might start agreeing with them and they'll all start congratulating one another on not seeing race.

I can say, **"THAT'S NOT OKAY!"**

You can start with simple and clear phrases like I often do, and then you can continue because folx will definitely be listening now!

"IT IS IMPORTANT TO SEE AND ACKNOWLEDGE AND UNDERSTAND THAT YOUR STUDENTS ARE DIFFERENT. BY WORKING TO ACTIVELY NOT SEE THE RACE/SKIN COLOR OF YOUR STUDENTS AND THEIR FAMILIES, YOU ARE DENYING THEM. YOU ARE DENYING THEM THEIR HISTORIES. YOU ARE DENYING THEM THEIR RACIAL AND ETHNIC BACKGROUND. YOU ARE BASICALLY SAYING YOU DON'T CARE ABOUT WHO THEY ARE. YOU ARE TRYING TO MAKE THEM THE SAME, AND FIT INTO THE IMAGINARY BOX. YOUR CLASSROOM ONLY TEACHES THE DOMINANT CULTURE OF WHITE SUPREMACY."

At this point, the person I interrupted will not be happy. A few other folx in the room won't be happy either. No one likes to be called out on their racism but it does need to happen. There will also be folx in the room who are listening and agreeing with you. You are not alone even if you are the only one using your voice and speaking truth at the moment.

It is okay if people are not happy with this. It is okay for them to be uncomfortable. Racism is not a comfortable existence for Black, Brown, and Indigenous Folx of the Global Majority.

COMFORT WILL NOT END RACISM.

There's a good chance the person I interrupted will deny they're racist. Or they'll try to dismiss me by saying something like, "Why do you always make this about race?" Or they might say something like, "You're being racist against white people." They might even say something like, "Are you saying I'm racist?" and try to turn the conversation into a discussion on how they couldn't possibly be racist because they're nice. Being racist against white people is not a thing. Remember, racism is personal prejudice AND the systemic misuse and abuse of power by institutions. So, I can have a prejudice against white people, but there is no system that has been put in place for centuries to keep white people oppressed. In our society, **REVERSE RACISM IS NOT REAL**. People will bring it up from time to time and you can remind them that personal prejudice is indeed real. However, institutions continue to misuse power to maintain a racist foundation against Black, Brown, and Indigenous folx. Therefore, the only people who benefit from that are white people. Contrary to the dictionary definition, racism is more than just the "personal prejudice" part of the equation.

"BY NOT ALLOWING YOURSELF TO SEE SOMEONE'S RACE, YOU ARE NOT SEEING THEM AS A WHOLE PERSON. YOU ARE LOOKING AT THEM THROUGH A SKEWED LENS. YOU SEE THEM ONLY HOW YOU WANT TO SEE THEM. YOU ARE LOOKING AT THEM THROUGH YOUR LENS OF COMFORT. YOU ARE NOT SEEING YOUR STUDENTS AND THEIR FAMILIES HOW THEY WANT TO AND NEED TO BE SEEN."

You can address their claim of not being racist with the quote from political activist, scholar, and author Angela Davis: "In a racist society, it's not enough to be nonracist, we must be anti-racist."

Then you can explain that we live in a racist society. Being nonracist will not change our current situation of racism. It

"IN A RACIST SOCIETY IT'S NOT ENOUGH TO BE NON RACIST WE MUST BE ANTI-RACIST"

may make you feel like you're a good person. But it, once again, reinforces racism. There is no action in being non-racist. You may be conscious of not saying racist statements and you yourself may feel like you are making a difference by sharing a quote from an African poet on social media. The reality is: inaction will do nothing other than maintain the old normal. Action, being anti-racist, will make change.

Yes, I often do talk about race and to some it may seem like I only ever talk about it. I will keep reminding those who are complicit with racism that it exists and isn't going away. I will continue to remind everyone that racism is causing great harm to the majority of the global population. I can do that. The more I practice it, the clearer I am with folx too.

SUPERPOWER 2: DANCING

I love dancing and will dance to just about any kind of music that is playing. Sometimes I'll sashay across the floor. Sometimes I'll do a terrible version of the robot, much to the embarrassment of folx around me. Sometimes I dance at parties with a lot of other people around. Sometimes I dance in the middle of the cereal aisle at the grocery store. Usually I dance at home with my family or by myself. Regardless, I love to dance.

Dancing is a different kind of superpower than my skills of interruption.

Taking a moment to express joy is something I don't always do. Taking care of myself isn't something I do often. Dancing allows me to pause, connect with myself and others, to express happiness, and be free. We all deserve to be free.

WE ALL
DESERVE
TO BE FREE

CHOOSING MY PATH

13

SOLIDARITY

TRUST YOURSELF IN THE MOMENT WHEN YOU CHOOSE TO STAND UP.

I was once in a room of over 100 people all discussing peace and social justice in education. Although we were in the same room, using the same words, our definitions and understandings were not all the same. This will happen.

Our backgrounds and knowledge, our growth and willingness to grow, and our positionality (or proximity to the dominant culture) affect how we interact with one another. It all allows us to use our voices or silence ourselves and others. It allows for our voices to be ignored or listened to.

I was triggered when a white woman (with authority and agency) mentioned, to the whole group, that social justice is an idea. My body immediately tensed up because I don't agree with that. Justice is not just an idea. It is a necessity for life. Our survival depends on it.

So I called her out. (We'll talk more about calling folx in and out in just a moment!) I used my superpower and spoke up in front of the whole group of people. I told her, "I'm going to call you out. Justice is not just an idea. It's a necessity for life." She immediately went into defense mode and I started to feel like I shouldn't have called her out. And definitely not in public. I started to regret

using my superpower until I looked beyond her. I noticed the other Folx of the Global Majority in the room. I saw all the other folx who exist outside of the imaginary box. They were nodding their heads, clapping and snapping. In that moment, I was accountable to them. They were what mattered. We mattered. Not the comfort of one.

There are moments when you will be made to feel like the comfort of one person is the most important over the safety and needs of many. You are accountable to moving the moment forward to justice and liberation. We are working toward an anti-racist society together.

My friend Britt explains the work of justice like this: Imagine we're all traveling along on the same lake. We start at the same place and

the end goal (of justice and liberation) is the same, but we have different means and paces to get to where we need to be.

Some folx are on a speedboat. They are moving fast, catching and making waves, with a clear path and purpose to get to the end goal of equity and justice. Their pace may seem too fast for some folx. That's okay.

Some folx are on a canoe. They're paddling along at a steady pace and getting to where they need to go. It's taking them longer than the folx in the speedboat. And that's okay. Sometimes they are thrown off their path because other elements and people have a big effect on their pace. They may also tire from this work of paddling along. At times, they may want to speed up or slow down.

Some folx are swimming. They are working at their own pace and are greatly affected by everything and everyone around them. They will fatigue if they keep swimming toward the goal without the help and support of others.

This is not your work alone. It can't be. Working in solidarity with others is an incredible way to take action and build collective power for change.

As you continue to wake up, grow into your superpowers, and take action, you will notice some folx will want to collaborate with you and others will distance themselves from you. You may find that you disagree with folx on how they want to disrupt or that the folx you are collaborating with may want to do things differently. This is okay. Know who you are. Have a vision. Listen to the folx who are impacted by your actions, and go forth.

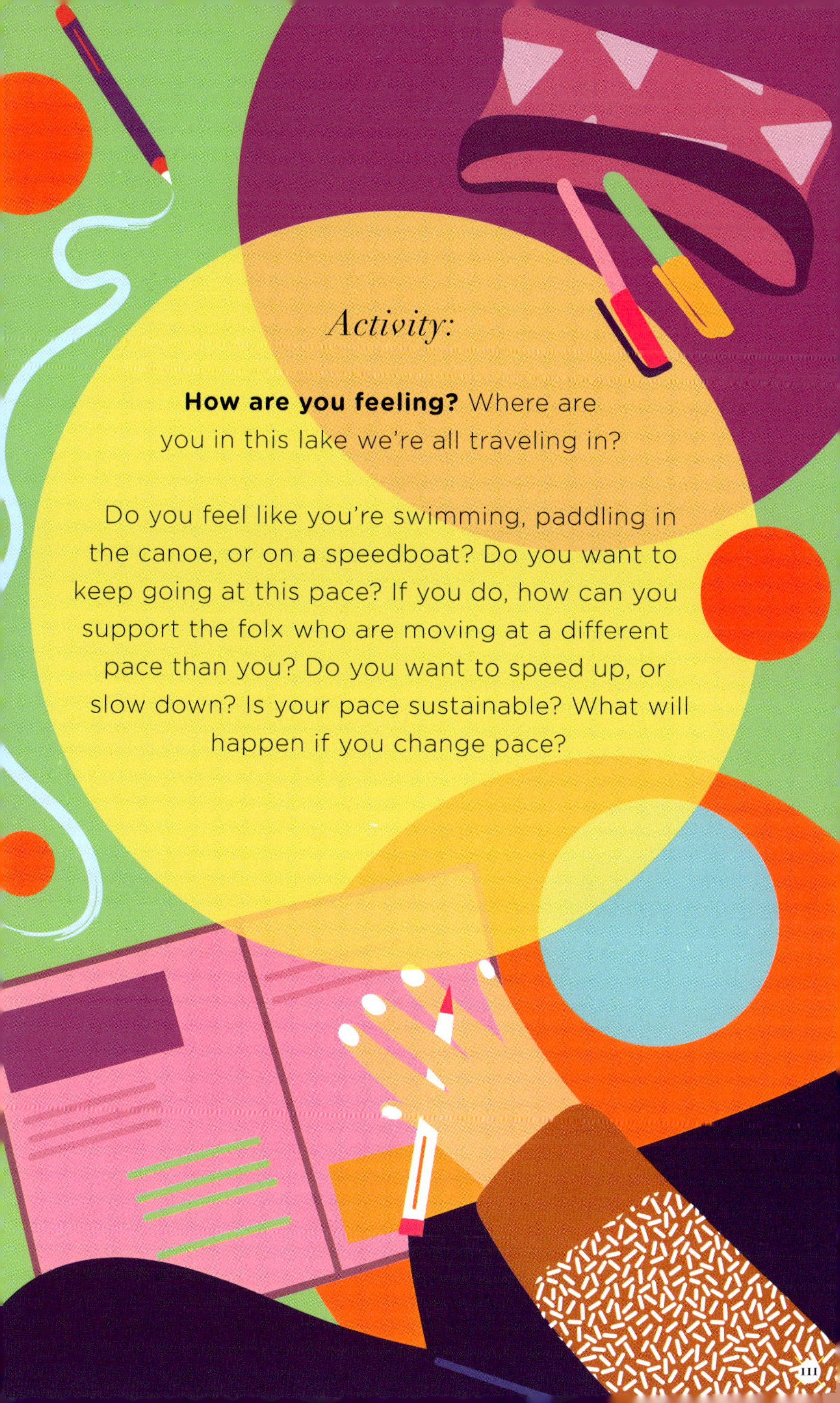

Activity:

How are you feeling? Where are you in this lake we're all traveling in?

Do you feel like you're swimming, paddling in the canoe, or on a speedboat? Do you want to keep going at this pace? If you do, how can you support the folx who are moving at a different pace than you? Do you want to speed up, or slow down? Is your pace sustainable? What will happen if you change pace?

CHOOSING MY PATH

14

CALLING IN AND CALLING OUT

WHAT DOES IT MEAN TO "CALL SOMEONE IN" OR "CALL SOMEONE OUT"? IS ONE OF THEM BETTER THAN THE OTHER?

If you call someone in, you circle back to a hurtful or oppressive comment they made in private. If you call someone out, you let them know their comment was hurtful in a public space. I'm going to be honest with you, I don't think one is better than the other. I personally call people out more than I call them in. It's what I'm more comfortable doing, but that doesn't mean it is what will work best for you.

Over the years I've learned that a lot of folx prefer to call others in and to be called in themselves, after someone says or does something that is harmful to an oppressed group.

For example, someone comments about a classmate who is Vietnamese American: "You don't want them on your track team, they'd be better in the science club."

If you are calling that person in, you can ask them to have lunch with you. You can tell them that they are perpetuating the **"myth of the model minority"** and that not all people who have Asian ancestry are math and science geniuses. You can explain that their comment over-generalized a large population of the world and lumps all folx from Asian countries into one big monolith of a people who are all the same. This is simply not true. Using the term Asian to describe all folx from Asian countries and ancestry does not acknowledge the vast and varied histories, cultures, and experiences of everyone.

To call someone in, you can also email or message them and explain why and how what they said is hurtful. You can send them articles and videos that explain how they perpetuated the stereotype that Asian folx are only good at math and science. And you can call them on the phone and let them know you heard what they said, that it bothered you because they were sharing misinformation and using a stereotype to set your Asian classmate apart from others.

Calling someone in can be a pretty effective way of working with someone to change their problematic behavior. They're more likely to hear what you are saying if it feels like a more gentle approach. It does require you to be compassionate and invest some of your time and energy.

If you choose to call that person out, other folx would be around and witnessing this interaction. You would probably say the things we just mentioned within earshot of other people.

Calling someone out can also be effective. It does require you to take a risk. You will be bringing attention to someone's oppressive and detrimental behavior. It allows for others to hear you and creates greater accountability as there's more than one person involved.

We will all have moments when we are the folx on the receiving end of a call-in or call-out. If you are the person who has just been called out, instead of bristling in defense, or getting upset, think about what the other person has just said. Hear them. Thank them for their comment and acknowledge you listened. Use that as a moment to teach yourself, open up dialogue, and dig deeper. This is how we all learn and move forward. As American poet, singer, and activist Maya Angelou said, "When you know better, do better."

Whether you choose to call someone in or call them out, know that it will feel messy and that it will be. You will question yourself, wondering if you should have done it or not. You will make mistakes from time to time—we all do. Every action you take gives you the chance to learn and grow. You've got this!

"WHEN
YOU KNOW
BETTER, DO
BETTER."

Before you call in or call out, grab your notebook and ask yourself the following questions. These might help you to decide how to go forth.

- Who has the power in this situation? The person I'm calling in/out, or me?

(If you have the power in this situation, consider calling them in.)

- Am I calling out a person or systemic behavior?

(If you're calling out systemic behavior or an institution, call them out.)

- How much energy and emotional labor am I able to share right now?

(If you don't have the energy or aren't willing to put in the emotional labor it takes to educate someone and work with them to change, consider calling them in with someone who can take on the work you are not able to do. I have a friend who helps me out when I don't have the capacity to educate white people on racial oppression.)

- Is this person likely to change their problematic behavior?

(If they are not, call them out. If this is someone you've called in before and they're still repeating their actions, call them out.)

- Who is in the room? Who am I accountable to in this moment? Am I centring the needs of myself or the group? What will happen if I call this behavior out? What will happen if I call this person in?

- What am I hoping to accomplish with this call -in or call-out?

IN THIS SECTION:
• SPENDING THAT PRIVILEGE
• ALLYSHIP
• BUILDING RELATIONSHIPS
• LOVE YOURSELF
• HOW WE GROW
• LIBERATION

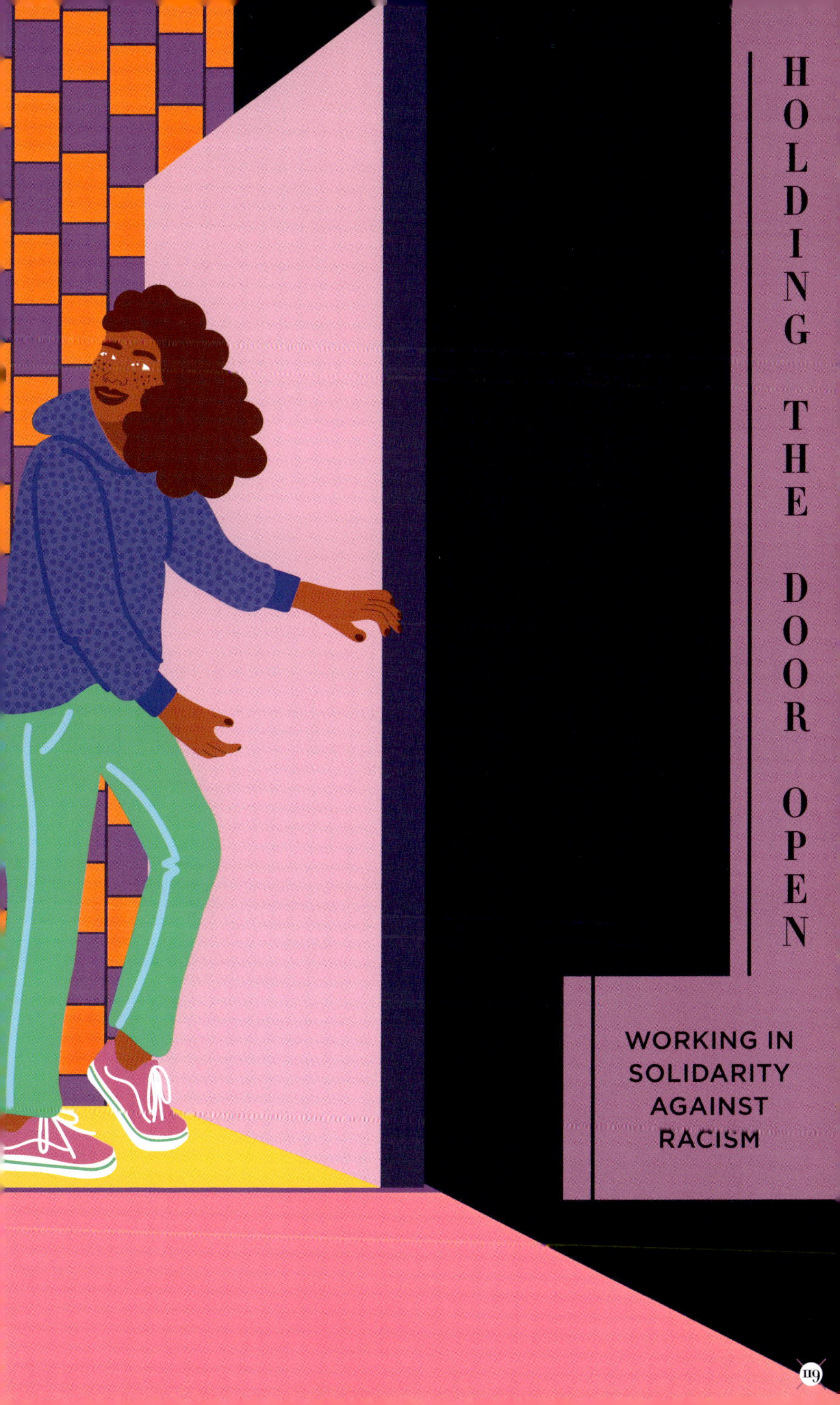
HOLDING THE DOOR OPEN
WORKING IN SOLIDARITY AGAINST RACISM

HOLDING THE DOOR OPEN

15

SPENDING THAT PRIVILEGE

YOU'RE AWAKE, REFLECTIVE, YOU'VE MADE A PLAN, AND YOU'RE READY TO TAKE ACTION. WE'RE NOT DONE THOUGH. WE ARE ACCOUNTABLE TO OURSELVES AND ONE ANOTHER.

But how do you go forth? How can you work in solidarity with others? When we bring our whole selves to the table we're bringing our different social identities, our oppression, our agency, our superiority and privilege, our experiences, and everything else that makes us who we are.

It is really important to acknowledge each person's wholeness. Sometimes your social identities will be the same as another's. Other times, your identities will complement someone else's and you—or they—will be able to use your privilege to support the other. And still, other times, your identities will be similar to another person's and you'll need to notice and acknowledge the subtle differences of your intersections. (Flip back to page 21 if you need a refresher on intersectionality.)

I know who I am. And I am still learning how all the parts of me make me a whole person in our society. I know that there are parts of me that exist outside of the box, and parts of me

that are inside the box or appeal to the dominant culture. My light skin makes people who reside inside the box comfortable. They see me and my loose curls and light shade of brown skin and see someone who could be like them. I don't speak in **African American Vernacular English (AAVE)** and so they are more open to listening. These are some parts of me that give me some access to whiteness. This proximity holds agency. Holding on to all of that privilege and power only serves the dominant culture. It allows for racism to continue on. I am not interested in that.

My adjacency to the dominant culture is my power in undoing it. And I can use this to keep the doors that have been opened for me wide open for those who are on the margins. You can do this too—especially if you are a person in the dominant culture. Black feminist and racial justice activist Brittany Packnett tells us to

To spend your privilege is to use your power and to change perceived normality.

"Using social media to spread awareness about underrepresented issues is a fine start. But as soon as you think you've spent enough privilege, that's a sign that it's time to spend some more," Packnett writes. If you are a cis male, use your voice to support and amplify trans folx and women and their many identities. If you are a person who has economic stability, use your position to redistribute resources and amplify those who are living in poverty. If you are white, spend your privilege by sharing the voices of Folx of the Global Majority, by stepping aside and giving them the space to lead, and by actually listening. Going into defense mode and centering your views when being called in or out upholds racism.

LISTEN AND LEARN FROM FOLX WHO ARE OUTSIDE THE BOX OF THE DOMINANT CULTURE.

COLLABORATE AND WORK IN SOLIDARITY WITH OTHERS.
BE MINDFUL TO NOT FALL INTO THE TRAPPINGS OF SAVIORISM OR CHARITY.
BLACK, INDIGENOUS, AND FOLX OF THE GLOBAL MAJORITY DO NOT NEED TO BE SAVED.
WE ALL NEED RACISM TO BE ERADICATED.

Activity:

Let's go back to the imaginary box.

In your notebook, draw a box. Inside of it write down the identities you hold that are a part of the dominant culture. On the outside of the box, write down your identities that are marginalized.

Those identities of yours that are inside the box are where you hold power. This is the privilege you can spend. Use the agency that comes with those identities to work in solidarity with folx who exist outside the box.

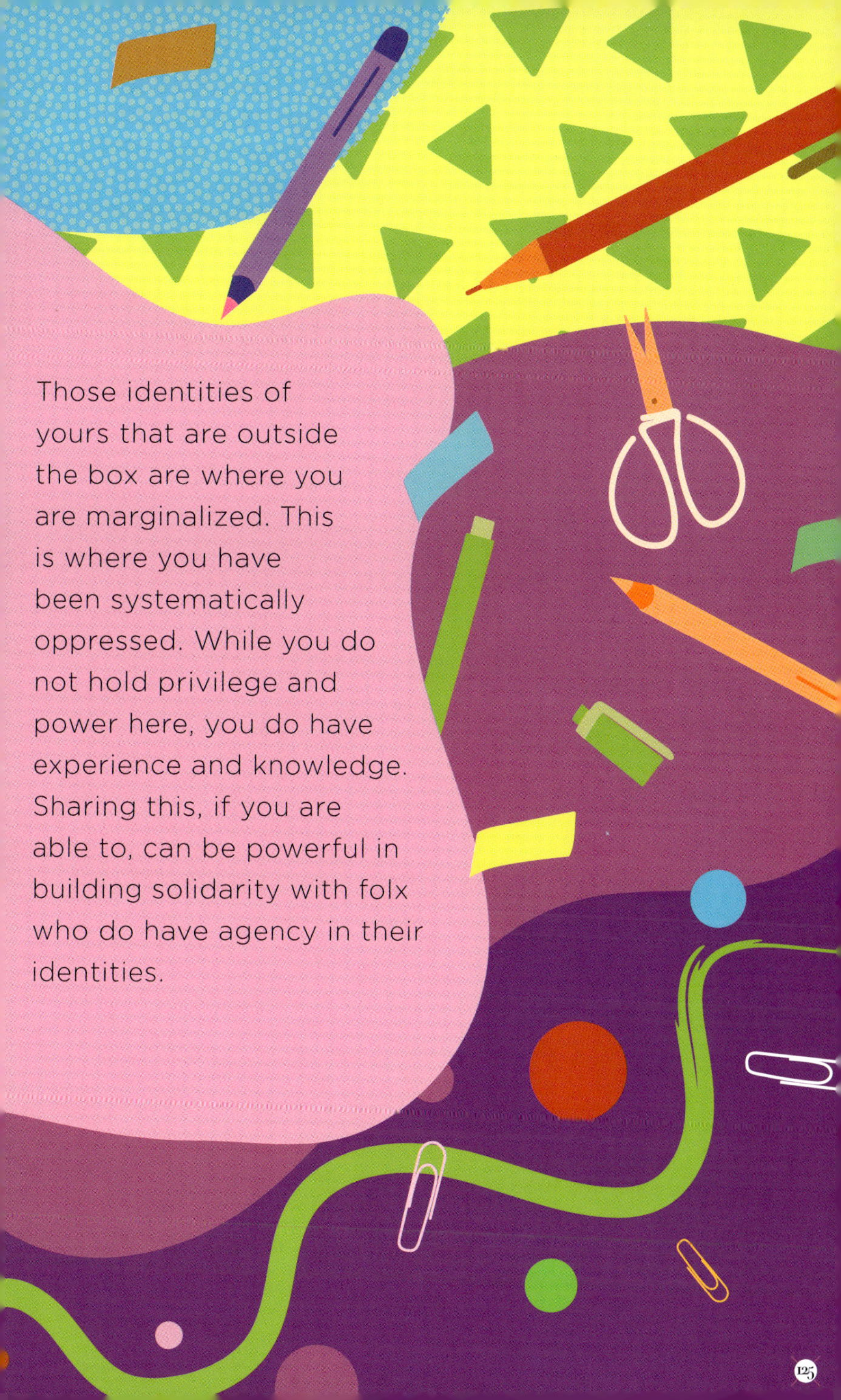

Those identities of yours that are outside the box are where you are marginalized. This is where you have been systematically oppressed. While you do not hold privilege and power here, you do have experience and knowledge. Sharing this, if you are able to, can be powerful in building solidarity with folx who do have agency in their identities.

HOLDING THE DOOR OPEN

16

ALLYSHIP

We are required to use our ability to see how we got here. We can analyze how racism was constructed and understand why we're still stuck in this smog. This will let us begin to clear the air. You may be ready to work with others to seek an anti-racist society. And now you're wondering what your role will be. There are lots of different terms for those who stand in solidarity, such as, ally, accomplice, partner, collaborator, and co-conspirator. They all have slightly different meanings. I prefer to use the terms accomplice and co-conspirator. They remind me to take risks in my anti-racism!

Pause for a moment, and reflect. (This is a good time to pull out your notebook!) What are some things you can do as an accomplice? How can you be an ally? Here are some things I've been working on:

- *Get angry. Racism harms us all.*
- *Keep learning. Continue to learn whatever you can so you can be*

a support.

- *Identify where you and your family hold influence in your spaces. Reni Eddo-Lodge, a British author, writes "White people: have conversations with white people about race." My friend Katie, a white educator from California, works with other white adults and children to dismantle the established culture of whiteness through workshops and lessons. When a white person questions me, Katie will do the work of talking with them so I don't have to. It seems like a small thing and we both know that because she's white, white people are more likely to listen to her. And if you are BIPoC notice where you may hold privilege. (Remember we all have different intersections!)*
- *Listen to Folx of the Global Majority and believe their stories. We are starting to see more representation in books, movies, and television, and the truth is it's a slow growth. About 7% of all new YA and children's books are written by Authors of the Global Majority.[31] Black, Indigenous, Asian, and Latinx folx are still greatly underrepresented in movies; close to 75% of speaking roles in films and television are given to white actors.[32] Go to movies that are directed by BIPoC, that portray Black and Brown folx in a positive way rather than as a stereotype, and celebrate Actors of the Global Majority. Read books by Black, Indigenous, and other People of Color who are sharing their #OwnVoices.*
- *Redistribute resources and support the work of BIPoC. You*

can donate funds or time to an organization led by and for Folx of the Global Majority or purchase goods (art, food, clothing) from Black- and Brown-owned businesses.

- *Stand up to police brutality: attend local protests and rallies when Black and Brown folx are harmed by the police. Bring your family, friends, teachers, and classmates. There really is strength and power in numbers when people gather together. Call people in power out.*
- *Identify racism. Always question it.*
- *Speak up and out. When you hear microaggressions, question them. If you hear someone ask another person, "What are you?," say something like, "Why do you need to know?" or "What are you really trying to ask?" or "Would you really want someone asking you what you are?" Call folx in.*
- *If you hear someone say, "You're pretty for a Black girl," say something like, "You're pretty racist. Just because your opinion of beauty is based on old Eurocentric beauty standards, doesn't mean you need to impose them on the rest of us. Keep your racist words to yourself and do better."*
- *If you hear someone refer to people as "illegals," you can tell them, "No one is illegal."*
- *If your teacher or the librarian continually highlights books and stories with white characters, written by white authors, you can tell them the facts shared in this section and remind them that only sharing one voice and one viewpoint (that of the dominant culture) forces us to not see ourselves in these stories, and tells us we don't matter and we don't belong. Advocate for changes in the way things have always been.*
- *If you hear someone say, "I'm not racist, but..." you can use your power of interruption to stop them from going any further, because they're probably going to say something racist.*
- *Racist bullying incidents are increasing in our schools. Be vigilant. Recognize when you hear racist phrases and see abuse. Report these to your teacher, counselor, principal, parents, or any adult you trust and they will help you. Check in with the person who is being bullied. Ask them if they would like to join you for lunch or walk them to class so they*

are not alone.

- *Notice when you are appreciating the culture and work of Black, Indigenous, or other Folx of Color and when you are appropriating it (taking it for your own use).*
- *Stand up against anti-immigrant attitudes and actions. You may hear family members or parents at school talk about how they "want their country back" and want to "make it great again," and you can disagree with them and call them out on their racism.*
- *Be mindful of the space you are taking up. Black, Indigenous, and other Folx of the Global Majority are continually silenced, talked over, and pushed aside. If you are BIPoC, take up space! Sit where you like. Go to the head of the line and bring other Black and Brown folx with you. Speak first. If you are white, step aside. You can help other white people to step aside too by sharing with them why you are not continuing to take up the space that was always given to you. You can also pause before you talk. The world is used to hearing the voices and stories of white people. Change the narrative.*
- *Check in with the Folx of the Global Majority. Living in a society that does not want you to exist is exhausting.*

Being an ally is life long work. As Yassmin Abdel-Magied, Sudanese Australian presenter and writer, shares, "Allyship is not something you can flick on or off when you have a Brown friend or a Black friend or a female friend. Remember to do it all the time." It's also messy at times and you will probably make mistakes. It happens. The important thing to do is to recognize when you're making a mistake, when you're not being a true accomplice, and shift out of that. The impact of your actions is lasting.

Allyship is not about you. It's not a performance or something you do to get more likes on social media. It's something you are working toward for a more just society.

This is something I am working on, always. Remember how my superpower is interrupting? There are times when that superpower actually doesn't come in handy. I interrupt myself from listening fully to the person talking. One of the things I am working on undoing in myself is believing that what I have to say is more important than what others are saying. Our society has conditioned me to think that, because I have light brown skin and a college education, I am superior to others. I am not. I am working on decentring myself from other people's stories. Listening when BIPoC talk is necessary for building strong coalitions. We all have a different story to tell and perspective to

share. This gives us a deeper understanding of how racism affects all of our lives.

I do want to be clear: it is not the job of Folx of the Global Majority to educate white people on their oppression. It is the job of white people to listen, learn, and grow.

Activity:

Ask yourself a few questions...

Who will you listen to?

What is it that you will listen to?

When will you listen and when will you interrupt?

How will you listen so that you are really and truly hearing what is being said?

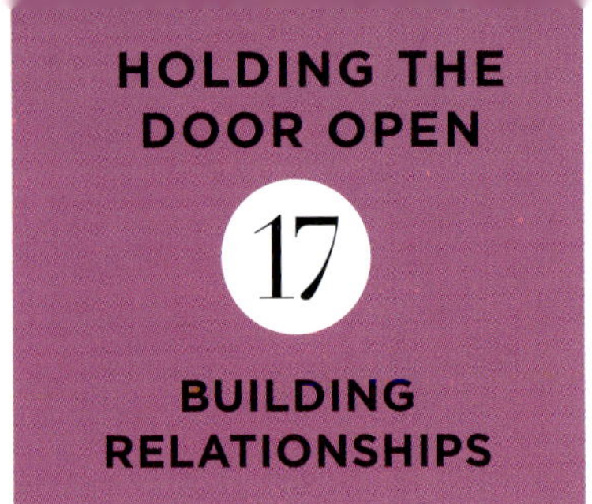

HOLDING THE DOOR OPEN

17

BUILDING RELATIONSHIPS

Anti-racism is lifelong work. What we take on started with our ancestors and what we leave behind will be carried on by those who come after us. As you make a commitment not only to disrupt racism, but also to actively break apart the foundation, you are honoring yourself and Folx of the Global Majority. You are building lifelong trusting relationships that are just and sustainable.

For a long time I tried to change a very slow-moving institution and move them toward having an anti-racist identity. I tried to do this alone. I shared a lot of my time and energy, knowledge and resources for free. I was exhausted, frustrated, angry, disheartened, and ready to give up.

And then I found "my people," thank goodness. I connected with other folx who do similar work in schools specifically around anti-racism. "My people" are those I can trust with my vision for justice. They help me to be a better person by challenging me and affirming me. They are folx who will always have a seat for me at the table.

We connected quickly because of the work we do and we were eager to have someone else who understands what we mean when we talk about racism.

I HOPE YOU FIND YOUR PEOPLE.

IT TAKES TIME TO BUILD THOSE SOLID, TRUSTING RELATIONSHIPS.

I'm not saying you have to become friends with everyone. I am advocating for you to work on creating equitable relationships with those you connect with.

UNDERSTAND YOUR PRIVILEGE

Intersectionality allows us to notice that, although we may share social identities, we are not the same and our experiences are different. I identify as a Black biracial cisgender woman. There are many other Black biracial cisgender women in the world. We share the labels for our identities, and some of our lived experiences will be similar and some will not.

All throughout my primary and secondary years my sister and I were in many of the advanced classes. We were even in the "gifted and talented" program, which allowed us to learn in a more exploratory way. We were raised by our white mom and our white family. Our school district labeled us as white. My teachers noticed my lighter skin color and believed I was better than my darker classmates. They showed this by holding higher expectations for me and encouraging me to pursue college preparatory classes. Many of my classmates were seen as troublemakers and were encouraged to join the military or pursue more technical classes.

As I've mentioned before, my proximity to whiteness has allowed me to travel more freely throughout the dominant culture. I am more palatable (acceptable) to white people. This privilege has ensured that I had more opportunities throughout my schooling—and beyond. Although we were a working-class family with immigrant roots, my sister and I were able to go to college and have careers we both enjoy.

Because of my closeness to the dominant culture, I can drive my car without having to worry that I will be pulled over for anything other than a brake light actually being out. I don't have to worry about being killed by the police officer who pulled me over like Philando Castile or taken to jail like Sandra Bland. People are more likely to believe me and trust me because of my privilege. I am no more special than anyone else because my Black skin is lighter.

Your privilege is something you don't often think about. It's often invisible to you until you take a moment to gain some insight and awareness into your whole self. You don't notice privileges because they are the parts of your identity that are considered normal (thanks to that imaginary box). We must actively work to understand our privileges across all of our various identities.

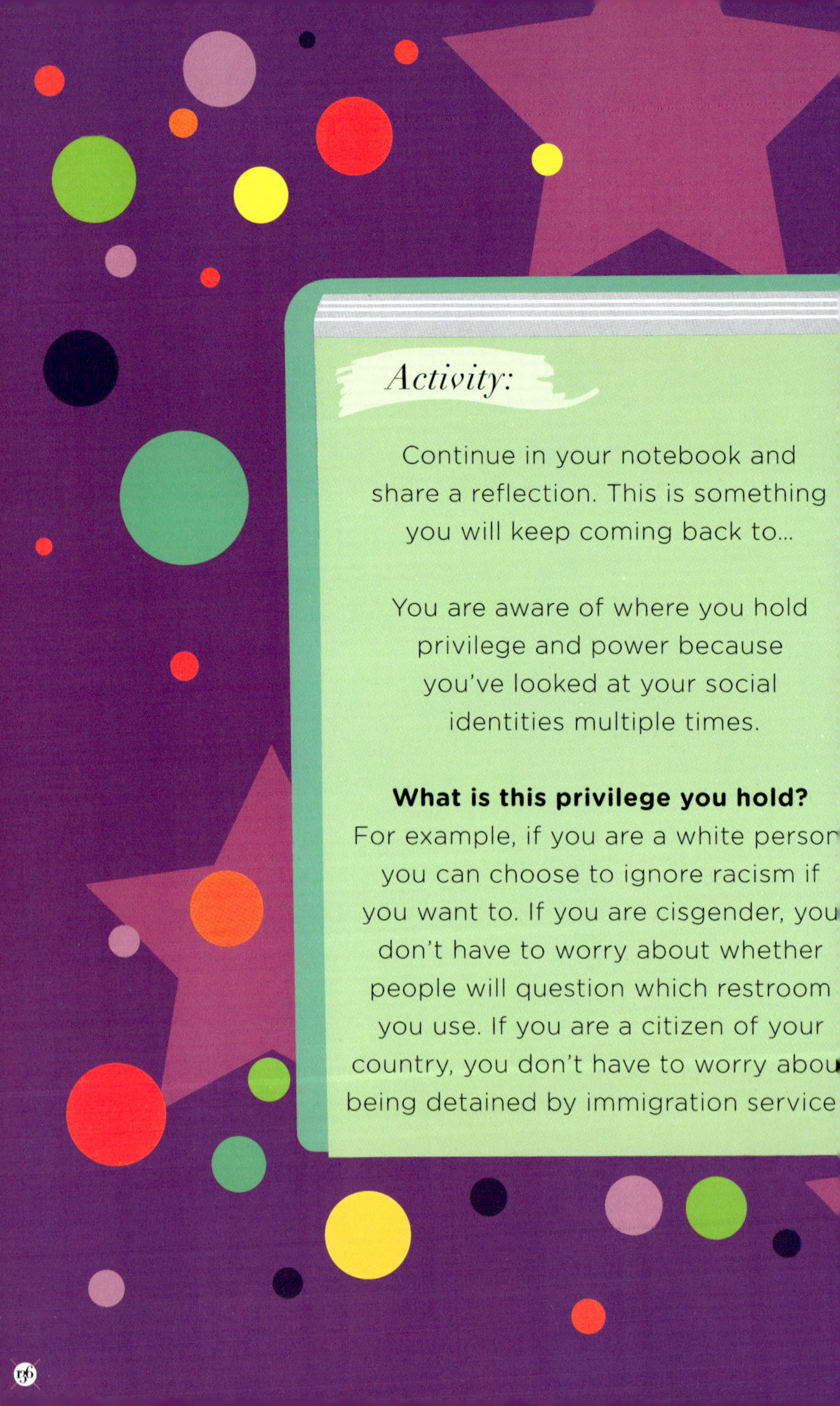

Activity:

Continue in your notebook and share a reflection. This is something you will keep coming back to...

You are aware of where you hold privilege and power because you've looked at your social identities multiple times.

What is this privilege you hold? For example, if you are a white person you can choose to ignore racism if you want to. If you are cisgender, you don't have to worry about whether people will question which restroom you use. If you are a citizen of your country, you don't have to worry about being detained by immigration service

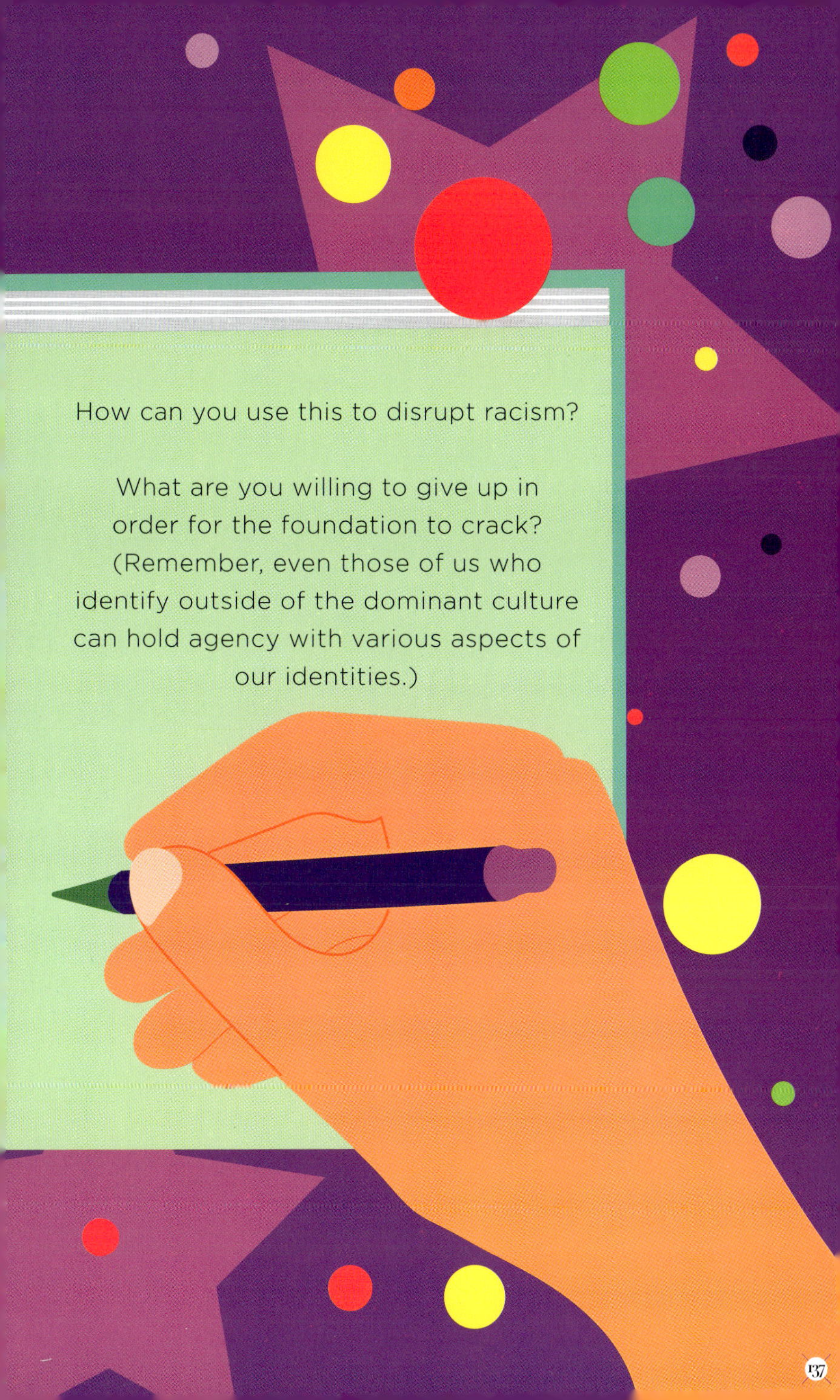

How can you use this to disrupt racism?

What are you willing to give up in order for the foundation to crack? (Remember, even those of us who identify outside of the dominant culture can hold agency with various aspects of our identities.)

Own who you are and who you are growing into. Love yourself and those around you.

It takes time to figure out who you are and what your role in anti-racism will be. This role will change. And so will you.

I have spent my whole life understanding who I am. My skin color hasn't changed, but my awareness of it has. So has my understanding of how my own history of being a descendant of both the colonizers and the colonized has impacted how society views me and how I see myself.

Knowing more about how I can take action and work in solidarity with others has helped me grow into figuring out what my role in anti-racism is. The moments when I can celebrate me have been moments when I am most ready and able to take on this work. James Baldwin wrote, in his book *The Fire Next Time*,

"TO ACCEPT ONE'S PAST—ONE'S HISTORY—IS NOT THE SAME THING AS DROWNING IN IT; IT IS LEARNING HOW TO USE IT. AN INVENTED PAST CAN NEVER BE USED; IT CRACKS AND CRUMBLES UNDER THE PRESSURES OF LIFE LIKE CLAY IN A SEASON OF DROUGHT."

BE YOUR
AUTHENTIC SELF.

I have got to own my past and not sit with who society conditioned me to become. And this goes for you too. Folx will be committed to trying to fit you into the box. They will tell you you're too young to make a difference, that you should focus on getting good grades and going to college. They may also tell you to be quiet, that your voice doesn't matter. Please do not listen. Believe in yourself. **I believe in you.**

Love yourself and set clear boundaries. It's okay to say no. You have to keep yourself safe and healthy. You know what you are able to do. You may need time to recharge or you may need to be with people to be energized. Anti-racism work can be very tiring. You're constantly working against the established norms, which have been set for centuries. You have not been in existence for as long. It's also okay to say yes and to take on this big work of dismantling racism! Take care of yourself. Stay hydrated. Get some good sleep. Read a good book. Spend time outside. Enjoy your time with family and friends. Celebrate you.

My people honor me for everything that I am. And I celebrate and honor them. We take pride in our achievements and support one another. We speak our truths and hear them. We learn from one another. We find joy whenever we can. We dance together. We love one another; it's how we resist.

Activity:

Remember this
and write it down...

Who are you? **Who is the YOU that you will celebrate?**

Who will you celebrate?

What boundaries can
you set?

Who am I?

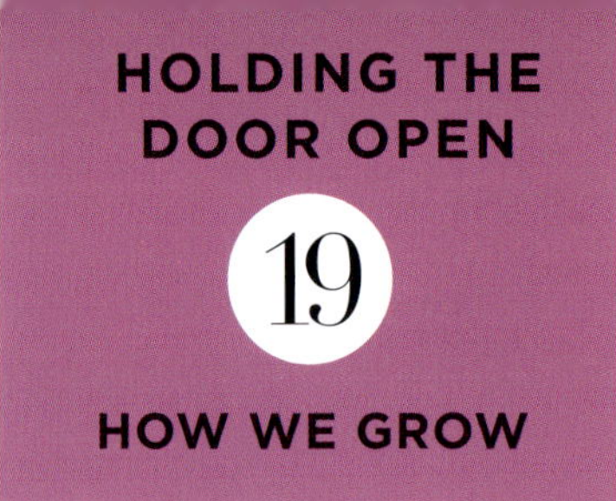

HOLDING THE DOOR OPEN

19

HOW WE GROW

DO NOT LET YOUR MISTAKES DEFINE YOU. I DON'T ALWAYS GET IT RIGHT. I AM STILL LEARNING; I AM ALWAYS LEARNING.

I tend to call folx out more than I call them in and that doesn't always work well for me when it comes to building relationships with others, especially when I am critiquing the person and not the system.

I once told a white male friend, in front of a room of other people, that the community is more likely to listen to him because he's white and male. (This is true.) I didn't need to make that comment in that space at that time. That call-out could have been a call-in.

We have known each other for years and he is working on being a better ally to Folx of the Global Majority. Calling him out like that put him on the defense and shut him down from a conversation that could have been more productive about the ways we can disrupt a system that always believes white men over Women of Color. We could have strategized for him to use his voice and power in his position to amplify Folx of the Global Majority and change what we've always done. The call-out stalled our working in solidarity with one another. It didn't allow us to have an open conversation about power and privilege.

I AM
ALWAYS
LEARNING.

I do want to be clear, I don't believe in catering to the comfort of white people in anti-racism.

WE GROW FROM OUR DISCOMFORT.

But it is important for me to understand that my actions have an impact. My intention when I called out my friend was to speak up and create awareness. The impact was that it took us longer to rebuild trust in each other and we didn't get to plan for how he can use his privilege to be a co-conspirator in changing the structure that places white men at the top of the hierarchy.

Apologize when you make a mistake. I don't do this as often as I should. I am stubborn and won't always admit when I am wrong. We have all been taught by the dominant culture that making a mistake makes us lesser members of society. This is simply not true. Everyone makes mistakes and we can learn from these so we can do better.

Know that even though your intentions were kind, the impact of your mistake is lasting and affects folx beyond yourself. Listen to others when they call you in and out. And learn from those moments and mistakes. Work on not repeating them and try not to let them deter you from doing the work.

Activity:

I imagine you're close to the end of your notebook. It's filling up! Let's take a moment to **acknowledge our mistakes** and grow from them.

What is a mistake you made when you chose to stand up and speak out? Or maybe your mistake was not speaking up?

What can you do differently next time you're in a similar situation?

"IF YOU HAVE COME HERE TO HELP ME, YOU ARE WASTING YOUR TIME. BUT IF YOU HAVE COME BECAUSE YOUR LIBERATION IS BOUND UP WITH MINE, THEN LET US WORK TOGETHER."

—*Lilla Watson, Indigenous Australian artist, activist, and academic*

Anti-racism is how we get free. Our liberation comes when we can express love and joy without fear and judgment and punishment. It comes when our institutions are for everybody, not just those who are in the dominant culture. When we who exist outside of the box have the resources we need to create our own institutions, we will all be free.

Racism is so deep within us. It is all around us and we have to be constantly aware of it so we don't get consumed by the smog. It is so easy to rest inside of it, especially if you benefit from the system that has been designed for you. (I'm speaking to you, white and white-passing folx.) We can't sit still and consciously breathe in racism anymore. We have to use our lens of anti-racism to help us see the world more clearly now, and we have each other.

Our liberation is bound together. I cannot dismantle this structure alone. You cannot break it down on your own. We are in this together. Our ability to disrupt our own **complicity** and the comfort of others has already begun to create little cracks within the system of racism.

Your awareness of yourself, your role in society, your privilege and power continues to grow. Your understanding of how racism came to be such an integral part of our global and local societies continues to expand. You are able to interrupt, disrupt, and take action with growing strategy and confidence. And you are ready to work in solidarity with others. You are a part of something big. You're writing your history and ours.

We are all on our own paths toward anti-racism and liberation. They will meet and eventually combine, but we have to travel along on our pathways first. You will get to know yourself well on this journey. And just when you think you know who you are, you'll discover something new.

Our paths are different because we are not the same. Our paths will meet because we are working for the same thing. It may feel uncomfortable when our different paths connect because our experiences and histories are different. We have different strengths and those will come in handy as we build a strong coalition of solidarity partners...

I AM LEAVING THE DOOR OPEN FOR YOU, PLEASE LEAVE IT OPEN FOR THE FOLX WHO COME AFTER US.

Activity:

1. What is your **vision for justice**?

What will it look like, feel like, and be like when we are all liberated from our racist ways of existing? How do you envision we will get there? What will be your role in this?

2. Find your song, poem, or piece of art. The one you can keep coming back to because it inspires you to keep going when you are tired. (Mine is Bob Marley's song "Babylon System.") Maybe yours is "Anti-Racist Youth," the poem on the next page.

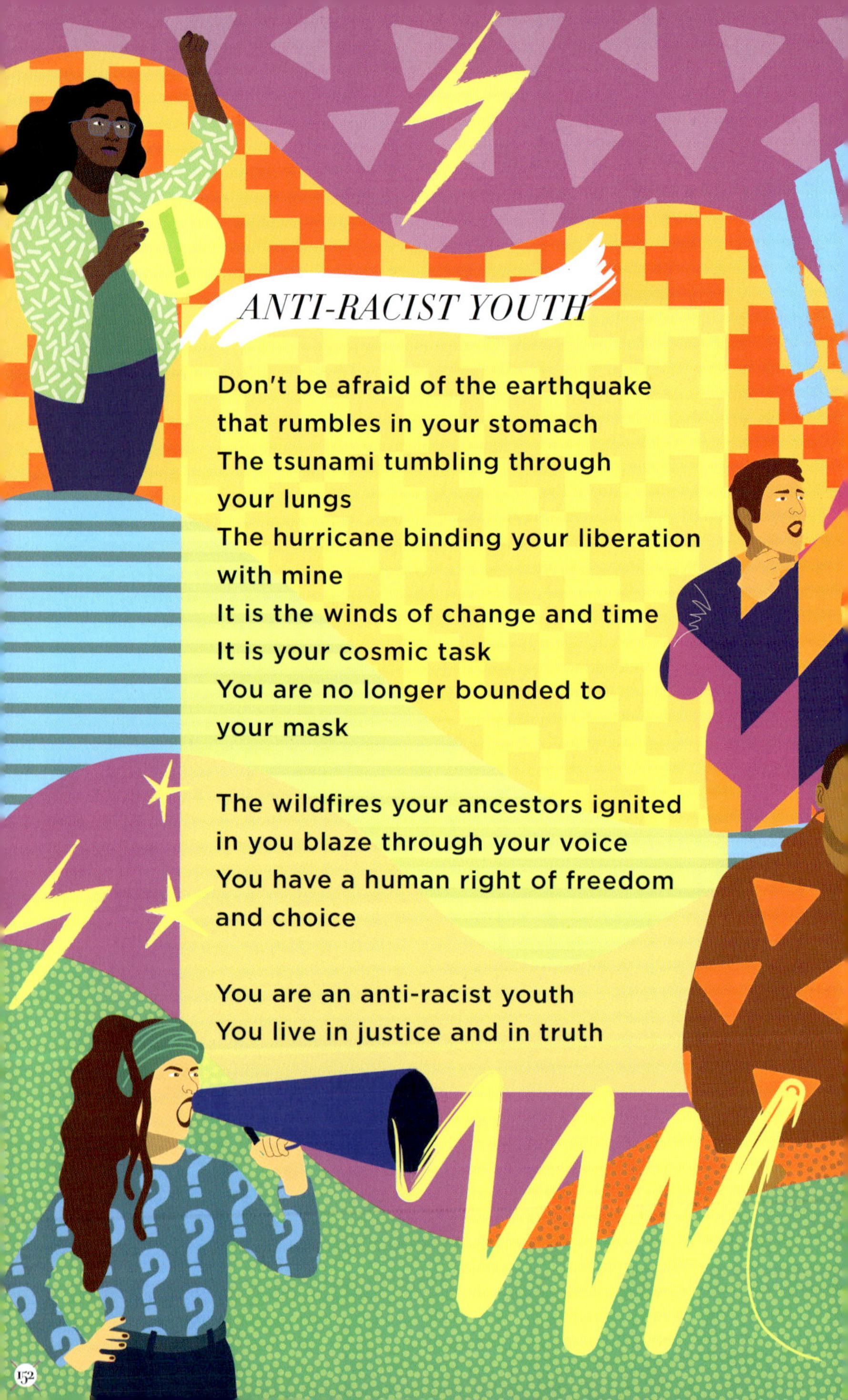

ANTI-RACIST YOUTH

Don't be afraid of the earthquake
that rumbles in your stomach
The tsunami tumbling through
your lungs
The hurricane binding your liberation
with mine
It is the winds of change and time
It is your cosmic task
You are no longer bounded to
your mask

The wildfires your ancestors ignited
in you blaze through your voice
You have a human right of freedom
and choice

You are an anti-racist youth
You live in justice and in truth

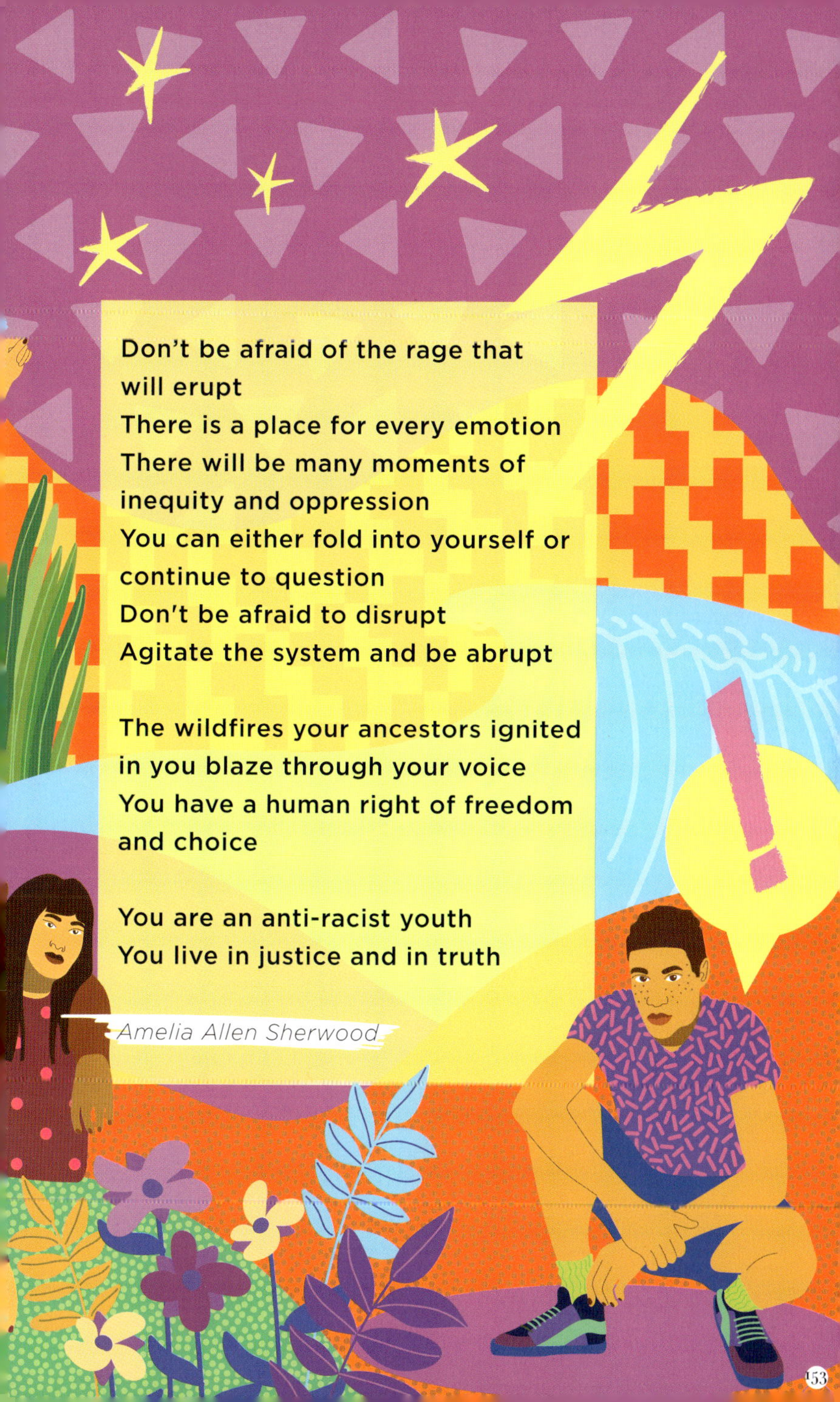

Don't be afraid of the rage that
will erupt
There is a place for every emotion
There will be many moments of
inequity and oppression
You can either fold into yourself or
continue to question
Don't be afraid to disrupt
Agitate the system and be abrupt

The wildfires your ancestors ignited
in you blaze through your voice
You have a human right of freedom
and choice

You are an anti-racist youth
You live in justice and in truth

Amelia Allen Sherwood

NOTES ON THE TEXT

1. Carl Linnaeus, the Swedish zoologist / botanist, is known as the "father of taxonomy" and is most famous for his book *Systema Naturae,* published in 1735. We still use his system of classifying plants and animals today, breaking down life into species, genus, family, etc. He also created categories for humans, as he was the first scientist to systematically categorize people along with animals. He created five categories for people that were mostly based on geography and the color of their skin. The four racialized groupings for people were: Europeanus (white), Americanus (reddish), Asiaticus (dark) and Africanus (Black), and the last group, Monstrosus, was the name given to folx with visible disabilities. Johann Blumenbach continued Linnaeus's work. He added a fifth grouping and noted that the people from the Caucus regions were, in his opinion, the most beautiful. The racial categories for people became: Caucasian, Malaysian, Ethiopian, American, and Mongolian. Blumenbach used physical beauty (which is subjective) to rank the different groups of people. He also believed that all humans were capable of reaching human perfection. This laid the groundwork for assimilation with the belief that folx could become more white and desirable over time.

2. I recognize that the term Latinx, while beautifully gender neutral, continues to enforce Euro-centricism. It is a common way to describe folx who live and have ancestors from countries and homes that were once colonized by the Spanish and other Latin-based language speaking places. The term Latinx is used to describe a large and varied group of people, just as Asian is used to describe folx from Afghanistan, Japan, Yemen, and all the people and places in between. I am working to acknowledge the many Indigenous folx who were colonized, and share that it is empowering to learn and reclaim Indigenous names: Taíno, Quichol, Q'eqchi', Zapotec, and all of the many Indigenous groups who were victims of colonization.

3. From "On the Natural Variety of Mankind," by J. Blumenbach, 1795.

4. I did not always refer to my race as Black biracial. I've used various words to describe my racialized identity: mixed, half-Black, other, biracial, multiracial, "half and half," and more. I don't love the word mixed to describe folx; I am a whole person. No one had to mix me up in a bowl to make me who I am. When I was presented with the choice to tick my race on forms in school, my options were limited. The choices were usually "Black, white, Asian, Native American, Native Hawaiian, and other." I often chose "other" because I could only tick one. "Other" did not sit well with me: it made me believe I didn't belong to any social group; it made me feel like I was alone. I don't love referring to myself as half of anything because it doesn't allow me to be my full self. Being just half of anything doesn't honor my wholeness. I prefer using Black biracial to describe my race.

5. University of Wisconsin-Milwaukee. "Children Are Not Colorblind: How Young Children Learn Race," E. N. Winkler, Ph.D.

6. European Agency for Fundamental Rights. "Being Black in the EU/Second European Union Minorities and Discrimination Survey," 2018

7. BBC News. "Grenfell Tower fire: Who were the victims," May 30, 2018.

8. *The Guardian.* "Khan attacks May on 'inhumane' treatment of Grenfell families," June 9, 2018.

9. *The Independent.* "The victims of Grenfell need answers and justice – but even more urgently they need homes," June 13, 2018.

10. *The Guardian.* "Housing market racism persists despite 'fair housing' laws," January 24, 2019.

11. *Wall Street Journal.* "Black Homeownership Drops to All-Time Low," July 15, 2019

12. *The Root.* "Flint: On This Day 4 Years Ago, the Water Crisis Started. The Water Is Still Not Safe," April 25, 2018.

13. *The Independent.* "Flint water crisis: Race 'was factor' in authorities' slow and misleading response," May 28, 2018.

14. "The Stephen Lawrence Inquiry," W. Macpherson, February 1999.

15. 30. US Department of Education. "The State of Racial Diversity in the Educator Workforce," July 2016.

16. 20. 21. *Black Stats: African Americans by the Numbers in the Twenty-First Century* by M. W. Morris

17. BBC News. "Five charts that tell the story of diversity in UK universities," May 24, 2018.

18. National Center for Education Statistics. "College Enrollment Rates" from The Condition of Education, 2019.

19. ThoughtCo, "How Racism in Health Care Has Affected Minorities Over the Years," March 18, 2017.

22. National Center for Biotechnology Information. "Implicit Racial/Ethnic Bias Among Health Care Professionals and Its Influence on Health Care Outcomes: A Systematic Review." By W. J. Hall, PhD, et al., 2015.

23. National Center for Biotechnology Information. "Racial bias in pain assessment and treatment recommendations, and false beliefs about biological differences between blacks and whites" by K. M. Hoffman, et al, 2015.

24. Medical News Today. "'Unconscious' Racial Bias among Doctors Linked to Poor Communication with Patients," March 16, 2012.

25. *American Journal of Public Health.* "The Influence of Implicit Bias on Treatment Recommendations for 4 Common Pediatric Conditions," by J. Sabin PhD, et al, 2011.

26. *The Atlantic.* "How Stand Your Ground Relates To George Zimmerman," T. Coates, July 16, 2013.

27. Inequality.org. "Facts: Racial Economic Inequality," [https://inequality.org/facts/racial-inequality/]

28. The Northern Plains Reservation Aid. History and Culture: Boarding schools.

29. *The Guardian.* "UK removed legal protection for Windrush Immigrants in 2014," April 16, 2018

31. Cooperative Children's Book Center. "Statistics on Multicultural Literature," 2017.

32. UCLA College, Social Sciences. "Hollywood Diversity Report 2018: Five Years of Progress and Missed Opportunities" Dr. D. Hunt et al.

GLOSSARY

AAVE - (African American Vernacular English) a dialect of English that is stigmatized due to the history of racism in America.

agency - your power to make effective change. It's your ability to make choices and decisions.

ancestral trauma - the transmission of trauma from survivors to the next generations.

anthropologist - a scientist who studies humans in both the past and present day. They study how people live and interact with one another, their language, their culture and traditions, as well as human behavior.

assimilate - to take on the customs, mannerisms, and ideas of a dominant group in order to fit in.

bias - your personal preference for, or against, an individual or group. It can interfere with your judgment.

BIPoC - Black, Indigenous, People of Color.

chattel slavery - enslavement. Folx (predominantly Black Africans) were considered property and their enslaved status was passed on from generation to generation.

cisgender - when your personal identity and gender expression correspond with the sex you were assigned at birth. The word can also be shortened to "cis", as in "cis female" or "cis male."

colonizer - a person who uses their power to dominate another group of people they deem inferior. Through colonization, which is when a group takes control over another, the colonizer uses violence and manipulation to gain and maintain power and control over land and resources.

complicity - when you go along with a harmful act. You are complicit when you go along with others who are committing an injustice.

discrimination - favoring one group over another in your thoughts and actions (both conscious and unconscious biases). It's the unjust treatment of folx who have different social identities than you.

ethnicity - your cultural heritage: languages, traditions, ancestral history. It is not the same as your race.

femme - a lesbian who identifies as having traditionally feminine traits.

Folx of the Global Majority - an empowering people-centered term that reminds folx that Black, Brown, and Indigenous people are (numerically) the majority of people in the world.

gender - the social construction, or performance, of your role in a society based on the dominant culture's creation of what is masculine and feminine. Your gender is not defined by the sex you were assigned at birth.

gender identity – your personal sense of who you are; it may be different or the same as the sex you were assigned at birth.

heterosexual – a person who is attracted to people of the opposite sex.

inferior – to be made to feel and believe that you are less than someone, that you are not good enough.

institutions – established laws, policies, customs, and procedures that are a part of our culture and way of being.

internalized – assimilating thoughts, behaviors, and actions of the dominant group into your own beliefs and values.

Latinx – the general, gender-neutral term for folx who are from Latin America and of Latin American descent. Folx who are from countries and places that were once colonized by Spain and Latin-based language countries are lumped into the term Latinx. (See p. 154)

marginalized – to be on the outside of the imaginary box of the dominant culture and treated as if you are insignificant and inferior. Marginalization is the purposeful disempowerment of folx that denies access to resources and power.

nationality – your membership in a country where you were born and/or where your citizenship resides.

neurodiverse – the term used to describe neurological differences (like ADHD, autism, dyslexia, Tourette's syndrome); acknowledges that these differences are from genetic variations, are often not visible, and that folx who are neurodiverse are not sick, badly behaved, or damaged.

neurotypical – people with typical development and intellectual ability.

nonbinary – folx who identify as having no gender, or a gender in-between (or beyond) being a man or a woman. It is a diverse category and not every nonbinary person feels the same way.

oppression – the systemic and systematic suppression of a group, or groups, by a group in power.

privilege – the benefits, advantages, and power given due to the social identities shared with the dominant culture. Privileges are granted and favored by institutions and social norms that were created by those in the imaginary box.

race – a socially constructed term that divides folx up based on their skin color and physical characteristics; it is not based on scientific fact and is not grounded in genetics.

sexual orientation – a social identity that corresponds with the gender you are attracted to.

social construction – an idea that has been created by society.

socioeconomic class – the socially constructed hierarchy based on economic wealth and mobility. Typically, the higher one's class, the greater influence and power one has.

solidarity – coming together with shared goals and actions and building a unified, lasting relationship with a person or group.

stereotype – a common oversimplified and/or distorted view of a person, thing, group, etc. that is not based on any fact.

superior – to believe you are better than someone else.

systematic – something methodical and planned.

systemic – something that happens throughout a whole system (and institution) over the course of time.

taxonomy – the classification of organisms and systems in nature.

transgender – someone whose gender identity differs from the gender they were assigned at birth.

white supremacy – the belief that white people are superior to those who are Black, Brown, Indigenous, and other Folx of the Global Majority because they are white.

SELECT BIBLIOGRAPHY

Books:

Adams, Maurianne et al (ed). *Readings for Diversity and Social Justice.*

Coates, Ta-Nehisi. *Between the World and Me.*

Coates, Ta-Nehisi. *We Were Eight Years in Power.*

Cooper, Brittney C. *Eloquent Rage: A Black Feminist Discovers Her Superpower.*

Davis, Angela Yvonne. *Freedom Is a Constant Struggle: Ferguson, Palestine, and the Foundations of a Movement.*

Davis, Angela Yvonne. *Women, Race & Class.*

Dunbar-Ortiz, Roxanne. *An Indigenous Peoples' History of the United States.*

Eddo-Lodge, Reni. *Why I'm No Longer Talking to White People About Race.*

Hurston, Zora Neale. *Barracoon.*

Kendi, Ibram X. *Stamped from the Beginning: The Definitive History of Racist Ideas in America.*

Lorde, Audre. *Sister Outsider: Essays and Speeches.*

Malavé, Idelisse, and Esti Giordani. *Latino Stats: American Hispanics by the Numbers.*

Mann, Charles C. *1491: New Revelations of the Americas Before Columbus*, 2019.

Morris, Monique W. *Black Stats: African Americans by the Numbers in the Twenty-First Century.*

Olusoga, David. *Black and British: A Forgotten History.*

Saad, Layla F. *Me and White Supremacy.*

Takaki , Ronald. *A Different Mirror: A History of Multicultural America.*

Tatum, Beverly Daniel. *"Why Are All the Black Kids Sitting Together in the Cafeteria?" And Other Conversations About Race.*

X, Malcolm, and Alex Haley. *The Autobiography of Malcolm X.*

Documentaries:

Bratt, Peter. "Dolores", 2018.

DuVernay, Ava. "13th", 2016.

Olsson, Göran. "The Black Power Mixtape 1967-1975", 2011.

Nelson Jr, Stanley. "The Black Panthers: Vanguard of the Revolution", PBS, 2015.

Peck, Raoul. "I Am Not Your Negro", 2017.

FURTHER READING

Non-fiction:

Gates Jr, Henry Louis, with Tonya Bolden. *Dark Sky Rising: Reconstruction and the Rise of Jim Crow.*

Guo, Winona, and Priya Vulchi. *Tell Me Who You Are: Sharing Our Stories of Race, Culture, and Identity.*

Lewis, John. *March* graphic novel series.

Loewen, James W. *Lies My Teacher Told Me: Young Reader's Edition.*

Stevenson, Bryan. *Just Mercy: A Story of Justice and Redemption.*

Wilson, Jamia, and Andrea Pippins. *Step Into Your Power*

Zinn, Howard. *A Young People's History of the United States.*

Fiction:

Ahmed, Samira. *Internment.*

Chanani, Nidhi. *Pashmina.*

Diaz, Natasha. *Color Me In.*

Dimaline, Cherie. *The Marrow Thieves.*

Parker Rhodes, Jewell. *Ghost Boys.*

Peña, Matt de la. *Mexican White Boy.*

Reynolds, Jason. *Long Way Down.*

Stone, Nic. *Dear Martin.*

Watson, Renee and Ellen Hagan. *Watch Us Rise.*

Yang, Gene Luen. *American Born Chinese.*

Zoboi, Ibi (ed). *Black Enough: Stories of Being Young & Black in America.*

First Published in the USA in 2020 by Frances Lincoln Children's Books, an imprint of The Quarto Group.
400 First Avenue North, Suite 400, Minneapolis, MN 55401, USA.
T (612) 344-8100 F (612) 344-8692 **www.QuartoKnows.com**

A catalog record for this book is available from the British Library.

ISBN 978-0-7112-4521-1

The illustrations were created digitally.
Set in Gotham Rounded.

Published by Katie Cotton
Designed by Karissa Santos
Edited by Katy Flint
Production by Nicolas Zeifman
Editorial assistance from Nick Whitney

Manufactured in Guangdong, China TT062021

14

MIX
Paper from responsible sources
FSC
www.fsc.org
FSC® C016973

Photographic acknowledgements: (pages 72–73, clockwise from top left) 1. Studio Portrait of Esau Prescott in Uniform, 1915 © Wisconsin Historical Society via Getty Images. 2. Sioux boys arrive at the Carlisle School, October 5, 1879 © CORBIS via Getty Images. 3. Jamaican immigrants arriving at Tilbury Docks in Essex, 22 June 1948 © Daily Herald Archive / SSPL / Getty Images. 4. Education, Segregation, USA, 1964, Queens, New York. A near deserted classroom with just five Black children attending, after a massive boycott by whites after the school had been included in the integration plan © Rolls Press / Popperfoto via Getty Images.
5. Portrait of nine-year-old African-American student Linda Brown as she poses outside Sumner Elementary School, Topeka, Kansas, 1953 © Carl Iwasaki / The LIFE Images Collection via Getty Images/Getty Images). 6. West Indian immigrants arrive at Victoria Station, London, after their journey from Southampton Docks, 1956 © Haywood Magee / Getty Images.